HAWTHORNE AND THE
HISTORICAL ROMANCE
OF NEW ENGLAND

. . . most difficult because we know
The failures of our fathers are the failures we shall make,
Their triumphs the triumphs we shall never have.
But remembering our fathers, we are compelled to praise,
And for their virtues hate them while we praise. . . .

Robert Penn Warren, *Brother to Dragons*

HAWTHORNE

AND THE HISTORICAL ROMANCE

OF NEW ENGLAND

MICHAEL DAVITT BELL

PRINCETON UNIVERSITY PRESS

PRINCETON, NEW JERSEY

1971

PS
1888
B4

Publication of this book has been aided by the
Princeton University Research Fund and by
the Whitney Darrow Publication Reserve Fund of
Princeton University Press

This book has been composed in Linotype Monticello
Printed in the United States of America by
Princeton University Press

WITH AFFECTION AND THANKS
THIS BOOK IS DEDICATED TO MY
MOTHER AND FATHER,

Marian Whieldon Bell
AND
Davitt Stranahan Bell

PREFACE

NATHANIEL HAWTHORNE was one of the most historically minded of our major novelists. From his first tales to his final unfinished romances he turned again and again to history—particularly to the early history of his native New England, which provided the material for his greatest novel and for many of his best tales. And yet it is a curious fact of Hawthorne scholarship that comparatively little sustained critical attention has been devoted to the specifically historical dimension of Hawthorne's historical fiction. One reason for this neglect is a tendency among critics to dismiss the historical in Hawthorne's fiction on the basis of a rigid distinction between "art" and "history." Since Hawthorne is an "artist," the argument runs, his works are "timeless" and should not be approached as if he were an "historian." Such critics apparently see no possibility for some middle ground, for an approach that can take "history" seriously as a part of "art."

And their fears that an "historical" approach will ignore "art" are partly justified by some of the criticism that *has* dealt with the historical dimension of Hawthorne's fiction. Some critics have approached Hawthorne as if he were indeed an historian—as if the validity or excellence of his fiction were a matter of historical accuracy. There is something to be said for this approach, since one expects of any artist some degree of fidelity to his material. But the approach has its limits, and they are soon reached. Beyond these limits concern for the historical "truth" of Hawthorne's treatment of Puritanism can lead to one of the more distressing commonplaces of Hawthorne criticism, the idea that Hawthorne was himself somehow a "Puritan." One is at something of a loss to know what this means. To be sure, Hawthorne is influenced by Puritanism. But to say that he *is* a Puritan is nonsense—as it would be nonsense to affirm that a child psychologist is a child. The way in which an author is influenced by his material is not the same thing as the way he treats his material.

In any case the present inquiry is directed toward the *treatment* of the Puritan past in Hawthorne's fiction. This is to say that I am concerned with Hawthorne's historical themes as they inform his tales and novels of seventeenth-century New England. Such an inquiry involves primarily not a comparison of Hawthorne's Puritans to the real Puritans or to Hawthorne's historical sources, but rather a close examination of the way the past is interpreted and presented in the works themselves.

It is sometimes useful, in deciding questions of interpretation, to compare Hawthorne's version of the New England past with his sources of information about that past. But the most useful comparison, it has seemed to me, is between Hawthorne's fictional version of the past and the treatments of that past in the fiction of Hawthorne's contemporaries. The thirteenth-century poet Jean Bodel classified medieval romance into "matters"—"De France, et de Bretagne, et de Rome la grant"—and his system has been generally adopted by literary historians. A similar system has, on occasion, been applied to the vast body of *American* historical romance.[1] In this study I assume such a system of "matters" and assume that one of the most important "matters" of American romance is the "Matter of New England." I assume further that just as one gains in understanding the *Morte d'Arthur* by viewing it in relation to the "Matter of Britain"—in relation to the other literary treatments of Arthurian legend—so one gains in understanding *The Scarlet Letter* and Hawthorne's tales of Puritan New England by viewing them in relation to the "Matter of New England."

When Hawthorne began in the 1820's to turn to the history of New England as material for fiction, there was widespread interest in the New England past, and in the American past generally, on the part of American writers. Between the serial publication of the anonymous *Salem Witchcraft* in 1820 and the publication of *The Scarlet Letter* in 1850 somewhere between 25 and 30 American romances were based, wholly or in part, on the history of seventeenth-century New England. These romances represent the work of many authors, known and less known, from Paulding and Cooper to Catharine Maria Sedgwick and Eliza Buckminster Lee. The popularity of their works, and of the ideas about New England history which these

[1] In the chapter in *The American Novel* (New York, 1921) entitled "The Three Matters of American Romance," Carl Van Doren classifies American historical fiction before Cooper in the three "matters" of "the Revolution, the Settlement, and the Frontier" (p. 17). A system of "matters" (although the term itself is not used) is the organizational basis of Ernest E. Leisy's *The American Historical Novel* (Norman, Okla., 1950).

works promulgate, formed the literary context in which Hawthorne formed his own contribution to the Matter of New England. Yet Hawthorne's relation to this general wave of interest in New England history has received very little attention in critical discussion of his historical fiction. It is a secondary purpose of the present study to rectify this omission by viewing Hawthorne's treatment of Puritanism in the context of the more conventional treatment of the Puritans in the fiction of Hawthorne's contemporaries.

Before I proceed I should make two general points about my use of the historical fiction of Hawthorne's contemporaries. First, as to the scope of my reading, I have read every American novel I could locate, published between 1820 and *The Scarlet Letter*, dealing with the history of seventeenth-century New England. I list 26 separate volumes in my bibliography. I am sure I have missed some titles, in spite of my efforts to be thorough; but I am just as sure that I have missed nothing of major importance—nothing, that is, by an author of the caliber of Cooper, Paulding, Motley, or Catharine Sedgwick. In any case I am sure my selection is representative of what was being done by Hawthorne's contemporaries, which is all the needs of this study require. For obvious reasons of space (and interest) I have not included detailed analyses of all of these works. And I have done my best to confine my remarks to generalizations about all of them or large groups of them, or to books which have some unique representative interest, such as Rufus Dawes's *Nix's Mate*.

My second point has to do with the kinds of rela-

tions I wish to establish between Hawthorne's historical fiction and that of his contemporaries. Hawthorne
undoubtedly read most of the novels listed in my bibliography, at least most of the big novels by the likes
of Cooper, Paulding, Whittier, Motley, Miss Sedgwick, or John Neal. But Hawthorne's relation to his
contemporaries is not primarily a matter of influence,
so that for the purposes of this study it is not necessary
to demonstrate which novels Hawthorne read, or
whether he actually read any of them. Hawthorne's
relation to such contemporaries as John Neal and
Catharine Sedgwick is most fundamentally a matter of
his being their contemporary. An early nineteenth-
century writer confronting the history of Puritan New
England, Hawthorne brought to that history many of
the same attitudes, prejudices, and problems brought
to that history by his less famous, and more conventional, contemporaries. The main purpose of relating
Hawthorne to those contemporaries, here, is to find out
just what the problems were that Hawthorne faced in
treating the Puritan past in fiction.

I have incurred debts of gratitude at virtually every
stage of developing and setting forth the ideas contained in this study. Many of my ideas about Hawthorne and his contemporaries germinated in the late
Perry Miller's great course on "Romanticism in American Literature," and I am deeply indebted to Professor
Miller's writings both on the American Puritans and
on the American Romantics. I owe thanks to President
Harold Martin of Union College, in whose Harvard
seminar on American historical fiction I first developed

PREFACE

my ideas about historical literature in general, and the historical romance of New England in particular. Professors Alan Heimert, Joel Porte, Richard Ludwig, Arlin Turner, and Richard Harter Fogle have been so kind as to read the manuscript at one stage or another. I express my appreciation to all of them for their many valuable reactions, suggestions, and criticisms, not to mention their patience. Many of the romances by Hawthorne's contemporaries were read at the Houghton Library, Harvard University, at the Boston Public Library, and at the Princeton University Library. I would like to thank the Research Council of Princeton University, who provided a grant for typing the manuscript, and Mrs. Helen Wright, who did the typing in her usual expert manner. I am also grateful for the helpful corrections and suggestions of Mrs. Eve Hanle. Finally I would like to thank my wife, Claudia Bell, whose enthusiasm and assistance made it much more pleasant for me to write this study, and whose criticisms have saved the reader from much obscurity, repetition, and confusion, which she herself had to endure.

CONTENTS

INTRODUCTION

THE TREATMENT OF
THE PAST

The appeal to national independence and national character is necessarily connected with a reawakening of national history, with memories of the past, of past greatness, of moments of national dishonour, whether this results in a progressive or reactionary ideology.

Georg Lukacs, *The Historical Novel*

I N 1825 WILLIAM CULLEN BRYANT announced to the New York Athenaeum:

Among the most remarkable of the influences of poetry is the exhibition of those analogies and correspondences which it beholds between the things of the moral and of the natural world. I refer to its adorning and illustrating each by the other—infusing a moral sentiment into natural objects, and bringing images of visible beauty and majesty to heighten the effect of moral sentiment.

Five years later William Ellery Channing wrote, in a similar vein:

Poetry is useful, by touching deep springs in the human soul; by giving voice to its more delicate feelings; by breathing out, and making more intelligible, the sympathy which subsists between the mind and the outward universe; by creating beautiful forms of manifestations for great moral truths. . . .
A writer, who would make [moral truth] visible and powerful, must strive to join an austere logic to a fervent eloquence; must place it in various lights; must create for it interesting forms; must wed it to beauty; . . . must show its correspondences with the outward world; perhaps must frame for it a vast machinery of fiction.

"Poetry" used elements of the "natural world" or "outward universe" to provide a "form" for "moral truths" or "moral sentiment," the terms "truth" and "sentiment" being used interchangeably and meaning something like what we mean by the "moral" of a story.

3

This was a symbolic theory of art; one drew one's materials from nature, but the ultimate test of art was the "moral truth" one managed to convey by means of this material.[1]

This doctrine is clearly an anticipation of Emersonian idealism; both Bryant and Channing, for instance, speak of "correspondences" between "moral truth" and "the outward world." The doctrine also had, in the earlier nineteenth century, an almost Elizabethan application to the writing of historical romance. In *The Defense of Poesy* Sidney had argued that one value of "poesy" was its ability to rearrange facts ("history") to correspond with or body forth moral truths ("philosophy"). "Whatsoever the philosopher saith should be done," Sidney wrote "[the peerless poet] gives a perfect picture of it by someone by whom he presupposeth it was done; so as he coupleth the general notion with the particular example." Or as William Gilmore Simms wrote, in 1845: "We care not so much for the intrinsic truth of history, as for the great moral truths." It was for these truths that the historical romancer was to "frame," in Channing's words, "a vast machinery of fiction." "He makes the imagination," Rufus Choate declared in 1833, ". . . he makes art, wit, eloquence, philosophy, and poetry, invention, a skilful plot, a spirited dialogue, a happy play, balance and rivalry of characters,—he makes all these contribute to embellish

[1] Bryant, *Lectures on Poetry*, in Parke Godwin (ed.), *Prose Writings*, New York, 1884, i, 19; *The Works of William E. Channing, D. D.*, Boston, 1841, i, 258, 265.

and recommend that essential, historical truth which is as the nucleus of the whole fair orb."[2]

But there is an important difference between Sidney's aesthetic and the aesthetic of the nineteenth-century historical romancers. The historian, for Sidney, was "tied, not to what should be but to what is, to the particular truth of things and not to the general reason of things." Historical events, so Sidney thought, were more often than not contradictory to moral truths; the historian was always at odds with the philosopher. For the historians and romancers of the early nineteenth century, however, no such contradiction obtained. History and philosophy were one, because history embodied moral truth. In the words of Bancroft: "The moral world is swayed by general laws. They extend not over inanimate nature only, but over man and nations; over the policy of rulers and the opinion of masses. Event succeeds event according to their influence." Just as the aesthetic of Bryant and Channing assumed a "correspondence" between the "outward world" and "moral truth," so the historical romancers assumed a correspondence between the events of history and the truths of philosophy.[3]

---

[2] Sidney, *The Defense of Poesy*, in Hyder E. Rollins and Herschel Baker (eds.), *The Renaissance in England*, Boston, 1954, p. 610; Simms, *Views and Reviews in American Literature, History and Fiction*, C. Hugh Holman (ed.), Cambridge, Mass., 1962, p. 38; Choate, "The Importance of Illustrating New-England History by a Series of Romances like the Waverley Novels," *The Life and Writings of Rufus Choate*, Boston, 1862, i, 340.

[3] Sidney, *The Defense of Poesy*, in Rollins and Baker, *The*

Thus the historical romancers who took their art seriously tended to develop their materials symbolically. Perhaps "representatively" would be a better word (as the Emersonian hero was to be a "representative man"); characters and events, in historical romance, really *are* a part or example of what they represent, since history was itself regarded as, in a sense, a *representation* of moral truth. "Scott," writes Georg Lukacs —and what he says is equally true of any serious historical romancer of this period—"endeavours to portray the struggles and antagonisms of history by means of characters who, in their psychology and destiny, always represent social trends and historical forces." Thus great historical figures are presented, not as Carlylean "heroes," but as "representative of an important and significant movement embracing large sections of the people." W. H. Gardiner said much the same thing in an 1822 review of Cooper's *The Spy.* "The power of creating interest in a work of fiction," he wrote, "so far as it arises from the development of character, lies in this generalizing principle which substitutes classes for individuals." This notion of the representative use of character lies at the heart of conventional characterization in early nineteenth-century historical romance.[4]

What, then, was the "principle," "sentiment," or "truth" behind the events of American history? The

---

Renaissance in England, p. 610; George Bancroft, *History of the United States*, 6 vols., New York, 1882, ii, 268.

[4] Lukacs, *The Historical Novel*, Hannah and Stanley Mitchell (trans.), Boston, 1962, pp. 34, 38; Gardiner, *North American Review* (hereinafter *NAR*), xv (1822), 251.

answer, in almost every case, was "progress." "The trust of our race that there is progress in human affairs," wrote Bancroft, "is warranted. . . . In every succession of revolutions, the cause of civilization and moral reform is advanced." While not all of Bancroft's contemporaries shared his ideas of what, precisely, "progress" entailed, they did agree for the most part that history was "progressive," or at least that it was linear. The natural form for expressing the linear movement of history, a form perfected by Scott, was the development of conflict—in the case of historical romance almost stylized conflict—between opposed forces of new and old, of progress and anti-progress. As David Levin puts it in his excellent study of American romantic historians: "the historian studied the age, looked for the banner of progress in any conflict, and supported the side fighting for it." Even if one saw history as tragic, rather than progressive, the form was the same. One simply "supported" the losing side. Not all nineteenth-century Americans agreed completely on just what (or whose) particular values were advanced under the "banner of progress." What a Jacksonian viewed as progressive a Whig would have been likely to view as dangerous. Still, in spite of these differences, there did exist a broad unanimity in support of the notion that something called "democracy" (or, even better, "liberty") was progressive, while something called "tyranny" (King George, if not necessarily Nicholas Biddle) was reactionary. Thus the romantic historian and historical romancer sought, in the past, a conflict which could be regarded as comprising a

7

battle between embryonic democracy and decadent authoritarianism.[5]

The romantic historian was, in essence, applying typology to history. "Typology," of course, is the theological doctrine that events of the Old Testament ("types") foreshadowed or predicted subsequent events in the New Testament ("anti-types"). The difference is that American historians in the earlier nineteenth century were seeking types, not of the coming of Christ, but of the triumph of "liberty." Each instance of the struggle between liberty and tyranny, each emergence of embryonic democracy, could be regarded as a type of the great culminating example of the victory of liberty over tyranny—the American Revolution. Thus, for example, Prescott proclaimed, while reviewing a volume of Bancroft's *History*, that the "principle" of American colonial history was "that tendency to independence" displayed throughout the two centuries preceding the Revolution. "It is this struggle with the mother-country," Prescott continued, "this constant assertion of the right of self-government, this tendency— feeble in its beginning, increasing with increasing age—towards republican institutions, which connects the Colonial history with that of the Union, and forms the true point of view from which it is to be regarded."[6]

The early history of New England was well suited to patriotic historical romance. The Puritan founding

[5] Bancroft, *History of the United States*, II, 269; David Levin, *History as Romantic Art*, New York, 1963, p. 29. My indebtedness to Professor Levin's book, in this introduction, is immense.

[6] Prescott, "Bancroft's United States" [1841], *Biographical and Critical Miscellanies*, London, 1845, pp. 269, 264.

fathers seemed especially designed for the cause of literary nationalism. For one thing, in the age of Scott they possessed obvious literary potential. "We had," wrote John Gorham Palfrey, casting a jealous eye on the reputation of the author of *Waverley*, "the same puritan character of stern, romantic enthusiasm of which, in the Scottish novels, such effective use is made, but impressed here on the whole face of society, and sublimed to a degree which it never elsewhere reached." What did Scott have, demanded a host of nationalist critics, that we did not have more of? Furthermore the Puritan founders seemed admirably suited to the secular typology of romantic American history. For had they not *begun* the long struggle for American liberty by defying tyrant-ridden England and establishing democracy in New England? The romantic historians dismissed or soft-pedaled the specifically religious motives of the Puritans who came to America. What mattered to the American nineteenth century was that the Puritan migration from England could be regarded as an early assertion of American liberty, as a type of the American Revolution. For instance, Daniel Webster, speaking at the two-hundredth anniversary of the landing at Plymouth, informed the assembled throng that it had gathered to commemorate "our attachment to those principles of civil and religious liberty, which [the Pilgrims] encountered the dangers of the ocean, the storms of heaven, the violence of savages, disease, exile, and famine, to enjoy and to establish." The Puritans, W. H. Gardiner believed, "fled to the wilderness for conscience' sake," founding

9

"the liberties of America on Plymouth rock." And in the romantic version of New England history the political motive that brought the Puritans to America continued to be the principle behind their actions after they arrived. "That spirit of liberty, which brought them hither," declared Rufus Choate, "was strengthened and reinforced, until at length . . . it burst forth here and wrought the wonders of the Revolution." One might compare to this the final sentence of Hawthorne's "Endicott and the Red Cross": "We look back through the mist of ages, and recognize in the rending of the Red Cross from New England's banner the first omen of that deliverance which our fathers consummated after the bones of the stern Puritan had lain more than a century in the dust."[7]

Nonetheless, there were real problems involved in applying this revolutionary reading to New England history. For had not these champions of liberty, these precursors of the American Revolution, expelled Roger Williams and Anne Hutchinson, clear representatives of individual liberty, as heretics? Had they not even hanged Quakers and so-called "witches"? These founders, who fled from persecution (the religious variety of "tyranny") to establish a nation in which persecution would no longer exist—had they not been the worst persecutors of all? This, to the romantic historians and

[7] Palfrey, *NAR*, xii (1821), 480; Webster, "The First Settlement of New England," *The Writings and Speeches of Daniel Webster*, 18 vols., Boston, 1903, i, 183; Gardiner, *NAR*, xv (1822), 256; Choate, "Colonial Age of New England," *Life and Writings*, i, 353; Hawthorne, *Works*, 15 vols., Boston, 1882-1891 (Standard Library Edition), i, 493-94.

historical romancers, was the great contradiction embedded in New England's early history. In romance after romance the reader is confronted with the lamentable fact that the Puritans fled persecution in England, only to establish it firmly in America. Even as early as 1792 Jeremy Belknap had had a character in *The Foresters*, loosely based on Roger Williams, demand of one of the Puritans: "Didst thou not come hitherunto for the sake of enjoying thy liberty, and did not I come to enjoy mine? Wherefore then dost thou assume to deprive me of the right which thou claimest for thyself?"[8]

A few historians, in the interest of historical accuracy, pointed out that the answer to the first question was "No," they did not come hitherunto for the sake of enjoying their liberty, at least not as the nineteenth century understood the word "liberty." The Puritans had not come to America to proclaim individual freedom, but rather to worship God in *one* particular way, a way sanctioned (as they thought) by the Bible but not by the Church of England. They objected, in the Church of England, not to the abstract notion of persecution, but to the concrete notion of what they held to be theological error. And they were as ready to use persecution to promote their own "holy" ends as the Anglicans were to promote theirs. The Puritans objected, not to the union of Church and State (which they took to be the natural order of things), but to the

---

[8] Belknap, *The Foresters, An American Tale*, Lewis A. Turlish (ed.), Gainesville, Fla., 1969 (Scholars' Facsimiles & Reprints), p. 34.

union of the state with the wrong church. "The principal emigrants," Bancroft observed, "were a community of believers, professing themselves to be fellow-members of Christ; not a school of philosophers, proclaiming universal toleration and inviting associates without regard to creed." The Puritans saw their migration more as a type of the New Jerusalem than of Yorktown. As John Winthrop had made clear in his "Speech to the General Court" in 1645, the only officially sanctioned "liberty" was "maintained and exercised in a way of subjection to authority."[9]

But the age continued to regard the Puritans as, in spirit (or "principle"), promoters of individual liberty. Even Bancroft, who could be so lucid about the actual goals of the "principal emigrants," continued to see the principle behind the migration in democratic terms. Puritanism, he wrote, "was Religion struggling in, with, and for the People; a war against tyranny and superstition. . . . It was its office to engraft the new institutions of popular energy upon the old European system of a feudal aristocracy and popular servitude. . . . Puritanism constituted not the Christian clergy, but the Christian people, the interpreter of the divine will; and the issue of Puritanism was popular sovereignty." Returning to the progressive interpretation of American Puritanism, Bancroft was forced as well to return to the great contradiction which that interpretation implied. Were not the Puritans themselves as

[9] Bancroft, *History of the United States*, i, 235; Winthrop, "Speech," in Perry Miller and Thomas H. Johnson (eds.), *The Puritans*, New York, 1938, p. 207.

much the agents as the foes of "tyranny and superstition"? "By degrees," Bancroft wrote of the New England Puritans, "the spirit of the establishment began
to subvert the fundamental principles of independency.
. . . The union of church and state was fast corrupting
both. . . . The uncompromising Congregationalists of
Massachusetts indulged the passions of their English
persecutors." In order to maintain their ideal of the
motives for the migration, American historians were
forced into the awkward position of having to present
the founding fathers as *betraying* that ideal. The romantic version of the migration, apparently so well
suited to the ennobling of the founders as patriotic
heroes, had the unfortunate side effect of presenting
those founders as betrayers of American liberty.[10]

This contradiction between the supposed advocacy
of liberty and the actual denial of it produced the central tension that informs the historical romance of New
England. The Americans of the earlier nineteenth century would not abandon their political ideal of the
migration, and the myth of betrayal, while it might
have resolved the historical contradiction, hardly provided a satisfactory basis for patriotic admiration.
American writers felt obligated by patriotic duty to
prove, as the title of one of Rufus Choate's patriotic
orations puts it, "The Age of the Pilgrims the Heroic
Period of Our History." But who, these writers were
forced to ask, were the "representative men" of this our
"heroic age"? Were they Winthrop, Cotton, Endicott,
and the like who, as the nineteenth century saw it,

[10] Bancroft, *History of the United States*, I, 317-18; *ibid.*, p. 312.

repudiated England only to imitate her tyranny? Or were the heroes those who *defied* the founders—Williams, Anne Hutchinson, the Quakers, and the "witches"? The problem for patriotic historical romancers was immense. They were torn between the patriotic impulse to idolize the founders as heroes and the romantic impulse to criticize them as enemies to independence and individual liberty. It was the task of the historical romancers who approached the early history of New England to attempt somehow to resolve this tension.

CHAPTER ONE

THE FOUNDING FATHERS

I regard it as a great thing for a nation to be able . . .
to look to an authentic race of founders, and a historical principle of institution, in which it may rationally
admire the realized idea of true heroism.

Rufus Choate, *The Age of the Pilgrims*
the Heroic Period of Our History

As FOUNDING FATHERS the Puritans were regarded by Hawthorne's contemporaries as national heroes; as persecutors they were regarded as narrow tyrants. The tension between the patriotic impulse to praise and the liberal impulse to criticize was central to the romantic treatment of the Puritan founders of New England. This tension is evident, first of all, in the balanced phrasing of most early nineteenth-century generalizations about the character of the Puritans. "We love to contemplate," wrote the anonymous author in the introduction to *The Salem Belle* (1842), "the piety and simplicity, while we deplore the superstition of those times. . . . Our fathers were not faultless, but as a community, a nobler race was never seen on the globe" [vii].[1] "In this enlightened and liberal age," Lydia Maria Child declared in *Hobomok* (1842), "it is perhaps too fashionable to look back upon those early sufferers in the cause of the Reformation, as a band of dark, discontented bigots. Without doubt, there were many broad, deep shadows in their characters, but there was likewise bold and powerful light" [6]. Many of the Puritans in the historical romances of New England are characterized by just such a balance or tension, as for example the "stern, sudden,

---

[1] Page references to the books under discussion will be given, throughout, in brackets following each quotation. A complete listing of the editions used will be found in the Bibliography of Primary Sources at the end of the volume.

choleric, but earnest, undaunted, untiring" Endicott, of John Lothrop Motley's *Merry-Mount* [ii, 118]. Motley's Endicott is at once bigot and hero. He is authoritarian and intolerant. Yet we are told that "altogether, the whole appearance of the personage . . . gave assurance of a man" [ii, 108]. A figure like Endicott, then, was equally praised and criticized. He embodied both of the age's attitudes toward the Puritan founders.

It is even more characteristic of the historical romance of the period, however, to polarize the supposedly contradictory aspects of Puritanism in opposed characters or groups of characters. One character or group represents the manly heroism of Puritanism, the other the narrow bigotry. Again, *Merry-Mount* furnishes a ready example, in the opposition of the Massachusetts governor, John Winthrop, and his deputy, Thomas Dudley. Winthrop, we are told, was "a tall, erect figure in the prime of manhood," whose magisterial garments "harmonized entirely with the simple and natural dignity which distinguished his presence." Even the recalcitrant criminal "could not look upon him without respect." "The whole countenance expressed elevation of sentiment, earnestness and decision, tempered with great gentleness, and somewhat overshadowed with melancholy." A reader familiar with Winthrop's political career might be surprised, finally, to learn that "the whole expression of the brow and eye would have struck an imaginative person as that of a man, whose thoughts were habitually and steadfastly directed to things beyond this world" [ii, 176]. Dudley is placed in clear opposition to Winthrop:

Well contrasted with Winthrop was the erect, military figure, and stern, rugged features of the deputy Dudley. The low-country soldier, the bigoted and intolerant Calvinist, the iron-handed and close-fisted financier, the severe magistrate, but the unflinching and heroic champion of a holy cause, were all represented in that massive and grizzled head, that furrowed countenance, that attitude of stern command. [ɪɪ, 176-77]

Here we have the same balance that characterized the description of Endicott, only now the heroic aspects are far outweighed and outnumbered by the repressive. As Dudley represents the bigotry and severity of Puritanism, Winthrop is freed (by the contrast) to represent the simplicity and noble piety of the founders.

The contrast between Dudley and Winthrop is not without historical justification.[2] Its importance, however, lies quite outside questions of historical accuracy. Motley's stylization and exaggeration of this opposition are more essentially a product of nineteenth-century predisposition than of seventeenth-century record. These characters represent a tension, not so much within Puritanism itself as within the nineteenth century's *view* of Puritanism. And in the nineteenth century this tension led, finally, to two stock character-types that appear again and again in the historical romance of New England. On the one hand there is the "narrow" Puritan who is usually presented much more critically than is Dudley in *Merry-Mount*. He is

[2] For example, Perry Miller and Thomas H. Johnson have written of Dudley: "A hard, single-minded man, he represents, as against Winthrop, the narrower and harsher features of early Puritanism." (*The Puritans*, New York, 1963, ɪ, xx.)

fanatical, often hypocritical, repressive, and even villainous. On the other hand there is the noble "founding father." He is no less "Puritan" than his opposite
number; at least he is in no sense opposed to the "stern"
tenets of Puritanism. The difference is that his narrowness is played down while his nobility is stressed. In
him, to borrow the phrase quoted from *The Salem
Belle*, the "piety and simplicity" of the founders are
developed while his opposite number, the fanatic, ab-
sorbs the faults, the "superstition," of our heroic age.
Sometimes, as in the case of Winthrop and Dudley,
these opposed character types are presented in pairs.
More often, however, they appear separately, each living a life of his own within the convention. The "narrow" Puritan is discussed at the beginning of the next
chapter. For the moment my remarks are confined to
the patriotic hero—the noble, simple, and pious "founding father."

The Noble Patriarch and the
Myth of Decline

The archetype of the founding father was John
Winthrop, first governor of the Massachusetts Bay
Colony. Mrs. Harriet Vaughan Cheney, in her inaus-
piciously titled *A Peep at the Pilgrims in Sixteen Hundred Thirty-Six* (1824), praises Winthrop's "popularity, the prudence and moderation of his character."
She sees his political career in terms of successful opposition to "the arts of the jealous, and the cabals of the
disaffected" [II, 23]. In a later work, *The Rivals of
Acadia* (1827), she praises the governor's "liberal

temper, and impartial administration," assuring the reader that "the voice of censure or applause had no power to draw him from the path of duty" [48-49]. In *Hope Leslie* (1827), Catharine Maria Sedgwick writes that Winthrop's "public life" is "well known to have been illustrated by the rare virtue of disinterested patriotism, and by . . . even and paternal goodness" [i, 212]. Furthermore, she writes earlier, "Mr. Winthrop is well known to have been a man of the most tender domestic affections and sympathies" [i, 9-10]. This figure, with his "disinterested patriotism" and especially his "paternal goodness," would seem to have more than a little in common with the popular idealization of George Washington, the Father of His Country. Winthrop's importance to the writers of the earlier nineteenth century stems in part from the fact that his *Journal*, published in part in 1790 and in full by James Savage in 1825, was an invaluable and often-consulted source of information on the early history of New England. Another important influence on these writers was the portrait of Winthrop as an embattled and disinterested leader in Thomas Hutchinson's *History of Massachusetts*, the first volume of which appeared in 1764. Hutchinson, in fact, concludes his portrait of the noble governor by calling him "the father of the country."[3]

But the patriarchal Winthrop is simply one of a great number of examples of a conventional stereotype of the founding fathers. However "narrow and mis-

[3] Thomas Hutchinson, *The History of Massachusetts from the First Settlement Thereof in 1628, until the Year 1750*, 2 vols., Boston, 1795, i, 142.

taken" their "conceptions of religious liberty," wrote
Eliza Buckminster Lee in *Naomi* (1848), "Winthrop
and his companions were as true, as pure, as heroic a
company as ever set foot on our sterile and severe
coast" [24-25]. Whatever their faults, the founders
were men, and men of integrity. "These primitive
statesmen . . . ," wrote another author two years after
Mrs. Lee, "had fortitude and self-reliance, and, in time
of difficulty or peril, stood up for the welfare of the
state like a line of cliffs against a tempestuous tide. The
traits of character here indicated were well represented
in the square cast of countenance and large physical
development of the colonial magistrates" [238]. This
is Hawthorne, describing the procession before the last
great scene in *The Scarlet Letter*.

Another part of this same description suggests that
in the figure of the founding father is embodied a
countermyth to the myth of historical progress discussed in my introduction. "It was an age," the narrator says of the seventeenth century, "when what we
call talent had far less consideration than now, but the
massive materials which produce stability and dignity
of character a great deal more" [237]. In some respects,
apparently, the nineteenth-century present represented
a decline from the standard of the founding fathers—
particularly with respect to integrity and manhood.
Hawthorne was hardly alone in sensing this decline.
James McHenry, in *The Spectre of the Forest* (1823),
declares that "the restless spirit of Yankyism which has
since actuated the minds of, no doubt, many of his
descendants, was unknown to the simple, unambitious

mind of the patriarchal puritan" [1, 23]. The "patriarchal" spirit of the founding fathers had given way to
a new "restless" spirit of ambition. The nineteenth-
century present had lost its respect for manly integrity.

We should not be surprised to find these historical
romancers expressing belief in both decline and progress, even when both views of history are expressed—
as is often the case—by the same writer. The ideas of
decline and progress are not as contradictory as they
might at first seem; both affirm change to be linear. The
difference between the two ideas is not a disagreement
over the nature of history but only a value judgment
about its direction, upward or downward. This difference is important to us here, however, since it lies behind the tension between the two attitudes toward the
original Puritans. On the one hand, ancestor worship
is clearly associated with a myth of decline—from those
ancestors. On the other hand, the myth of progress just
as clearly requires some sort of repudiation, however
clandestine, of one's ancestors. The figure of the noble
founding father is ultimately a dramatic representation
of a feeling that America has declined since the seventeenth century. The figure of the narrow Puritan represents the progressive nineteenth century's criticism
of an unenlightened earlier age. The nineteenth-century
romancers' portraits of the founders are of little value
to the student of seventeenth-century history. But they
are of great value to the student of nineteenth-century
literature. They tell us a great deal, not only about what
the romancers thought of their own time, but also what
they thought about time in general, about the direction

of history. And among these thoughts about history was a myth of historical decline from the character of the founding fathers.[4] Whatever the faults of these fathers, according to the Mrs. Cheney who so enthusiastically praised Winthrop, theirs was an age in which "ambition had not . . . assumed the mask of patriotism, nor were the unprincipled and licentious, elevated to the 'high places' of the land" [*Peep*, I, 55]. Again and again the age of the founders is described as an age of heroic piety, of manly principle, a Golden Age after which the nineteenth-century present seems puny and insignificant.

Perhaps the fullest picture of this idealized age, and of the decline which regrettably succeeded it, is to be found in James Fenimore Cooper's 1829 romance, *The Wept of Wish-Ton-Wish*. The first part of this book takes place in 1660 at the isolated settlement of Wish-Ton-Wish in Connecticut. This frontier society is dominated by the patriarchal Mark Heathcote, who is

---

[4] Already in the seventeenth century the myth of decline from the founders had gained currency in the sermons described by Perry Miller as "jeremiads." (*The New England Mind, From Colony to Province*, Boston, 1961, pp. 27-39.) Many nineteenth-century romancers were aware of these sermons and of their insistence on declension from the piety and nobility of the founders. But I think influence, if it exists here at all, is quite indirect—a matter of inherited temperament rather than direct borrowing. The myth of decline was certainly as natural to the nineteenth century as to the seventeenth. As Wesley Frank Craven says of the "jeremiad" in *The Legend of the Founding Fathers* (New York, 1956, p. 15): "The theme at least will strike you as a familiar one, for surely most of us have caught the orator's suggestion on the Fourth of July that a generation of giants has been succeeded by a lesser breed of men."

joined briefly by an old companion, one of the regicide judges of Charles I. The community is attacked by Indians and burned to the ground. But the few settlers have saved themselves by hiding in a well underneath the blockhouse. They emerge after the departure of the savages to raise a prayer of thanksgiving. Heathcote, true as always to his Christian principles, refuses to countenance any talk of vengeance on the Indians. The second part of the book takes place fifteen years later, during the Indian uprising known as King Philip's War. The Heathcote settlement is now a good-sized town, and its founder, who is very old and seldom seen, has passed his authority to his altogether less impressive son, Content Heathcote. Similarly, Mark's paternal religious authority has been passed on to a hypocritical minister, significantly named Meek Wolfe. During one of Wolfe's canting sermons the old regicide—associated, like Mark Heathcote, with the older, simpler world—appears to warn of an Indian attack. The Indians are beaten off, but the Heathcote family is captured by an Indian named Conanchet. They are released, because old Mark had treated Conanchet well years before. Yet after Conanchet departs, Meek Wolfe forsakes Mark's principle of forswearing vengeance and urges retaliation. Even Content, at last, abandons his father's principles. Conanchet is captured and turned over to the Mohicans, in full knowledge that they will execute him. Thus Content is directly responsible for the death of a man who had recently saved the entire Heathcote family. This is clearly no longer the world of the original Heathcote or of the stranger who had, as Conanchet has expressed it, "taken the scalp of a great chief" [395].

The Wept of Wish-Ton-Wish is a stark portrayal of decline—decline from principle to expediency, from founding father to succeeding son.[5] Mark Heathcote has the authority to maintain his principles. His successors have neither his authority nor his principles. The principle itself—the forswearing of unnecessary vengeance—is important, but it is finally less important, in the book's scheme of values, than the simple fact that one should hold to one's principles whatever they are. Perhaps the most important characteristic of the "principled" characters in *The Wept*—Mark and the regicide stranger—is the air of authority which surrounds these two men and most clearly distinguishes them from the next generation. When the stranger interrupts Meek Wolfe to warn of the Indian attack, we are struck, not by what he says or does, but rather by the tone of his "deep, authoritative voice" [324], which contrasts so clearly with the "ambiguous qualifications" [323] that characterize the minister's sermon. When the regicide first appears at Wish-Ton-Wish, he and Mark discuss matters of importance in secret, while the family is suffered to wait in an outer room. "That deep reverence," we are told, "which the years, paternity, and character of the grandfather had inspired, prevented all from approaching the quarter of the apart-

---

[5] I am indebted, in my discussion of Cooper's romance, to John P. McWilliams's excellent study of Cooper's works, "A Law for Democracy: Cooper and the American Frontier," unpublished Ph.D. thesis, Harvard University, 1967.

ment nearest the room they had left" [48]. The ability to inspire such "reverence" is not passed on to Mark's son.

In spite of its elevating patriarchal past over democratic present this is not an anti-democratic book. Cooper's *Wept of Wish-Ton-Wish* portrays not a decline from feudalism to democracy but a decline from a noble liberty to a base liberty. The liberty by which Mark lives, and which he lives to defend, is the liberty to maintain his own principles by his own authority. Content's liberty, by contrast, is simply expedience— the liberty to ignore principle. A superannuated Mark lives on into the world of Content as a reminder to this newer world of what it has lost. And loss and collapse dominate the closing pages of the book. We are told that the settlement has prospered even down to the present, but a detailed description reveals decline—an "old and decaying" orchard, "the ruins of the blockhouse" [471]. A final grim effect is provided by couching the concluding remarks on the characters in the form of a survey of their graves, a device used 21 years later by Hawthorne. The mood of these concluding pages simply reinforces the point already made, that American history is the record of a declension from the integrity of the founding fathers, an integrity represented in Cooper's romance by the figures of Mark Heathcote and the unidentified regicide.

The Regicide

This regicide merits our more particular attention, for he is something of a staple legendary figure in the historical romance of Puritan New England. A regicide judge appears in eight of the two dozen or so romances written about Puritan New England between 1820 and 1850; in five of these he is a major character.[6] Three of the men who signed the death warrant of Charles I fled to America following the restoration of his son to the English throne. They were John Dixwell, Edward Whalley, and William Goffe. Dixwell, whom the new king never knew to be in America, is not mentioned in the historical romances of New England. Whalley, a first cousin of Cromwell, and his son-in-law Goffe fled to Massachusetts in 1660. After a brief respite in Cambridge they fled to New Haven where they were protected by the minister John Davenport and the governor of New Haven (still distinct from Connecticut), William Leete. Pursued by the royal agents, Thomas Kirk and Thomas Kellond, they hid for a month in the "Judges' Cave" on West Rock in New Haven. Finally, in 1664, they fled to Hadley, a new settlement on the Connecticut frontier. Whalley probably died about 1674. The final regicide tradition, first recorded by Hutchinson, has to do with an Indian attack on Hadley during King Philip's War in 1675. The townspeople, taken completely by surprise, were

---

[6] The five works in which a regicide is a major character are: James McHenry's *The Spectre of the Forest* (1823), the anonymous *Witch of New England* (1824), Cooper's *Wept* (1829), Delia Bacon's *The Regicides* (1834), and William Henry Herbert's *The Fair Puritan* (1844-1845). The three works in which a regicide has a minor role are William Leete Stone's *Mercy Disborough* (1834), the anonymous *Salem Belle* (1842), and James Kirke Paulding's *The Puritan and His Daughter* (1849).

falling back before the savages when suddenly they were rallied by the mysterious appearance of a stern old man who led them to victory. This old man, so the tradition goes, was William Goffe.[7]

The tradition of the attack on Hadley, as we have seen, bore fruit in the work of Cooper—in the old regicide's interruption of Meek Wolfe's sermon to warn of approaching Indians.[8] But the material was first tapped for fiction not by an American, but by Sir Walter Scott. In Scott's *Peveril of the Peak* Major Bridgenorth recounts to Julian Peveril an incident that he witnessed in a New England town "more than thirty miles from Boston." During an Indian attack the townspeople were rallied by "a tall man, of a reverend appearance. . . . I never saw anything more august than his features, overshadowed by locks of grey hair, which mingled with a long beard of the same color." This stranger, Bridgenorth confides, was none other than the regicide, "Richard [*sic*] Whalley." Bridgenorth disapproves of the execution of King Charles, but he admires the stern nobility of the regicide, a nobility apparently lacking in present-day Restoration England. "Perhaps," he concludes, "his voice may be heard in the field once more, should England need one of her noblest hearts." Julian has evoked this story from Major Bridgenorth by ex-

[7] The fullest account of the lives of the regicides available in the early nineteenth century was Ezra Stiles's *History of Three of the Judges of Charles I*, Hartford, 1794.

[8] For another account of the Hadley tradition in nineteenth-century American fiction, see G. Harrison Orians, "The Angel of Hadley in Fiction. A Study of the Sources of Hawthorne's 'The Grey Champion,' " *American Literature*, IV (1932), 256-69.

claiming: "It must be a noble sight . . . to behold the slumbering energies of a great mind awakened into energy, and to see it assume the authority which is its due over spirits more meanly endowed."[9] For both Scott and Cooper the old regicide represents the hope, in contrast to a period of decline and moral uncertainty, that the "authority" and "energy" of the old Puritans is not dead but only "slumbering." For Cooper the regicide is all the more important for his association with America's founding fathers.

The Hadley tradition is revived, briefly, in James Kirke Paulding's *The Puritan and His Daughter* (1849). The people of a frontier town are falling back before the Indians "when suddenly there appeared among them an aged man, with long white beard, and head whitened with the snows of many winters, who called on them in a voice that seemed accustomed to obedience, and arrested their retreat" [ii, 172-73]. The tide is turned, the battle won, and, as the Indians retreat, the old man disappears. "It was," the author concludes, "the last appearance of one who had sat in judgment on a king" [ii, 173]. Here again we find the age and natural authority seen already in Scott and Cooper. To some extent, then, the figure of the regicide is simply another form of the conventional founding father, superannuated but sublime, representative of a fiercer, nobler, and manlier age.

But these regicide judges who had, in the picturesque phrase of Cooper's Conanchet, "taken the scalp

[9] Sir Walter Scott, *Peveril of the Peak*, *The Edinburgh Waverley*, Edinburgh, 1902, xxviii, 246, 248, 252, 245-46.

of a great chief" also offered unique symbolic oppor-
tunities to the writer of American historical romance.
It was hard to see the founding fathers, however manly,
as in any way prefiguring the glorious American Revolution. They had stood firmly for their own principles.
But these principles were, if anything, quite the opposite of those notions of universal liberty of opinion associated, in the popular mind of the nineteenth century,
with 1776. The regicides had a much clearer typological link with the War for Independence: they had
defied, and finally executed, the King of England. To be
sure, their motives for this act were no closer to the
supposedly egalitarian principles of the Revolution than
were the motives of those who originally left England
for New England. But they wrote and did little to dis-
tract the attention of romantic historians from their
great central action, the deposing of the King.

Historical romance writers were not long in perceiv-
ing the symbolic possibilities of the regicides as types
of the American revolutionary spirit. In 1824 an anonymous work entitled *The Witch of New England* presented Whalley as an old man living on the outskirts
of an unnamed town. He announces that he is persecuted by one who "will never cease to persecute the
friends of a pure and free government" [133]. The
persecutor is obviously Charles II; but it is not clear
whether the "pure and free government" is England's
or America's. The latter idea is supported by his proph-
esying in a long speech to the hero a future age when
"this land" will be independent [134-35]. Delia Bacon's
long tale, *The Regicides* (1831), deals primarily with

the actions of the colonists of New Haven in protecting Whalley and Goffe from the royal agents Kirk and Kellond. Pitting patriotic Americans against British intruders, *The Regicides* reminds one more of the romances of the American Revolution than of the history of the seventeenth century. The book is built on the contrast between the "air of undaunted effrontery" of the royal agents and the purity and nobility of the Americans—of the protectors of those judges who "had boldly stood up for the rights of conscience and freedom in their native land, even until the blood of a royal martyr had stained their path" [32]. The prerevolutionary message of the book is clear in Governor Leete's announcement of the assembly's refusal to assist the royal agents. "The assembly," he declares, "is the supreme power of this colony, and by no means a *subordinate* institution" [41].

It is not necessary to rehearse the plots of these romances. Suffice it to say that the regicides are repeatedly associated with the American Revolution and with American liberty. For instance, the anonymous author of *The Salem Belle* (1842) writes of Goffe: "his ashes rest in a land where no kingly prerogative tramples with its iron foot on the sacred rights of man, and where the blessed vision that shone so brightly on his eye, is a living and glorious reality" [75]. The regicide in Paulding's *The Puritan and His Daughter* says to the young hero: "I look to a new world, and a new people, to do justice to my memory. . . . The people who are daily flocking hither are destined to be free" [ii, 159]. It is important to note that these regicides, in acquiring an association with the independent future, do not lose their association with the patriarchal past. This regicide in Paulding's book, who prophesies a "new world" of freedom, speaks "in a voice that seemed accustomed to obedience," and he is described as "an aged man, with long white beard, and head whitened with the snows of many winters" [II, 172-73]. The patriarchal role of the regicides is even clearer in their being so often near ancestors of the principal characters of these romances. In *The Spectre of the Forest*, *The Salem Belle*, *The Fair Puritan*, and *The Regicides* the hero or heroine is a child or grandchild of one of the regicide judges. These judges are quite literally founding fathers. In the figure of the regicide it was possible, at least apparently, to fuse the supposedly democratic principles of the American Revolution with the patriarchal austerity of the Puritan founders. What results from this fusion is a curiously *old* idea of revolution. We are accustomed to think of revolution as an activity primarily of the young. It is a peculiar feature of this literature that it regards revolution not as a young *rejection* but as an old *assertion* of authority. The prophetic voice of the regicide speaks not from the approaching future but from the vanishing past.

Rufus Dawes and the Revolution of the Patriarchs

The events of the history of seventeenth-century New England, like the severe character of the Puritan founders, presented enormous problems for the progressive, typological historical romancer. Where, amid the banishments, suppressions, and hangings that marked this history was one to find the germs, the types of American democracy? Such germs were usually found among those banished, suppressed, and hanged. What seems primarily to have interested the historical romancers about New England Puritanism was its *violations* of the principles of American liberty. The great theme of the Matter of New England was not the conflict between Puritanism and external tyranny, but the conflict within Puritanism itself between the forces of tyranny and the forces of liberty. Again and again the nineteenth-century romancers turned to the suppression of dissidents, the banishment of Anglicans, the slaughter of Indians, and the hanging of Quakers and witches.

Nonetheless, there was one obvious example of an historical contest between Puritanism and external tyranny which did not go unchronicled. In 1689, as news of the Glorious Revolution in England began to reach New England, the people of Boston overthrew and imprisoned Edmund Andros, the repressive royal governor of New England. In his place they reestablished the authority of the old charter governor, Simon Bradstreet, now eighty-six years old. For Americans of the earlier nineteenth century this event betokened more than simply colonial reaction to the accession of William and Mary. The larger meaning was clear, for example, to George Bancroft. "Boston," he wrote of 1689, "was the centre of the revolution which now spread to the Chesapeake; in less than a century it will begin a revolution for humanity, and rouse a spirit of power to emancipate the world."[10] The Revolution of 1689 was first treated in fiction in 1834, in Hawthorne's tale, "The Gray Champion." Five years later Rufus Dawes made it the principal subject of his full-scale romance, *Nix's Mate*. And the revolution is included, finally, in Henry W. Herbert's *The Fair Puritan* (1844-1845). Dawes's *Nix's Mate* is particularly interesting at this point and merits rather detailed discussion, because it indicates clearly the problems raised, for the American writer of the early nineteenth century, by the issues discussed in this chapter. *Nix's Mate* is a failure. But in its failure we can see what happens when the myth of progress, of revolutionary typology, collides with the countermyth of historical decline. This collision finds its fictional embodiment in the tragic confrontation of Dawes's young Byronic hero, Edward Fitzvassal, with the patriarchal society of Puritan Boston.

The story begins as Fitzvassal, a pirate, arrives in Boston in search of his mother. He is, it turns out, the illegitimate son of one of Governor Andros's closest friends, Edmund Vassal. While seeking his mother, Fitzvassal falls in love with a girl named Grace Wilmer, daughter of another close friend of the governor, but he discovers too late that Grace is pledged to another. Fitzvassal's hatred for his father is cemented by discovering his abandoned mother dying in a damp basement just in time to hear "that most appalling of

[10] George Bancroft, *History of the United States*, 6 vols., New York, 1882, I, 601.

all sounds, the death-rattle" [I, 181]. Meanwhile, the Boston in which these events are transpiring is filling with a revolutionary spirit clearly intended to anticipate 1776. "Measures were in rapid progress," we are told, "for effecting a revolution in some degree analogous to that which in less than a hundred years after, was achieved by the sons of liberty" [I, 91]. "The Revolution of 1689," Dawes writes, "begun and finished in Massachusetts, was the parent of the memorable one that nearly a century after succeeded, and made way for the emancipation of the world" [II, 237]. Fitzvassal becomes very much a part of this gathering revolution. Exclaiming to a crowd of sailors in a tavern, "I hate tyranny," he concludes with an insurrectionist toast: "let us drink confusion to all tyranny and rascality on sea and on shore" [I, 69-71].

But before the successful ending of the revolution, Fitzvassal has a chilling experience which seems at first totally unrelated to his revolutionary activities. While illegally boarding a merchant ship he kills a man in combat and then discovers he has slain his father, Edmund Vassal. This murder is obscured, however, by the events leading up to the successful deposition of Andros. Fitzvassal's pirate ship is instrumental in securing Boston harbor for the foes of Andros. In consideration for his service to the cause Fitzvassal is given a conspicuous place at the celebration of the success—the restoration of the old charter and of the old charter governor, Bradstreet. But in the midst of this celebration officers enter to arrest the young man on charges of piracy. He pleads guilty and is sentenced to death by the government he has helped to install. Just as a pardon is being brought in, he dies from poison taken to avoid the humiliation of public execution. This sudden turn of events (even the fact that Fitzvassal is a pirate is withheld until well into the second volume) is more than a little shocking. The ending is dominated by the contradiction between Dawes's apparent sympathy for his hero and the fate to which he consigns him—by the contradiction between Fitzvassal's apparent status as a patriotic hero and the sudden death to which he is condemned because of his "real" status as a villainous pirate.

Dawes's striking ambivalence toward his hero is accompanied by an even more striking ambivalence toward history, and especially toward revolution. On the one hand, at least up to the arrest of Fitzvassal, *Nix's Mate* appears to be progressive both in ideology and structure. At the close, a revolution continually compared to 1776 is brought to a successful conclusion. What is more, the book is filled with explicit statements about the progressive nature of history. The establishment of Protestantism in America is seen as "a step . . . in human progress which could not admit of retrogression" [I, 113]. An old philosopher anticipates the "antitype of that progress which I see sketched out before me" [I, 140]. Even the heroine looks ahead to a time "when the veil that hangs between the spiritual and natural worlds will be withdrawn, . . . an era, in short, when the true democratic principle will be understood, and just conceptions of equality entertained" [II, 16]. On the other hand, there are a number of statements in

the book that qualify, if they do not absolutely contra-
dict, Dawes's generally progressive notion of history.
For instance, in the midst of describing the celebration
of victory over Andros the author laments the fact that
the commercial spirit is destroying (in 1839) the great
old "spirit" of America [ii, 240]. In this sense revolution is an ideal of the past, rather than the future. History is regarded, not as continual progress, but as inevitable decline. And this decline, we learn, is from the
greatness of the fathers. "A very few of the original
stock remained," writes Dawes as he begins a rather
different sort of comparison between 1689 and 1776,
"and as they passed to the world of spirits, their example was gradually forgotten: just as the disinterested
patriotism of seventy-six is becoming only a theme for
the historian, as the heroes of that epoch are fading
from our memory" [ii, 193].

This statement suggests, among other things, the
figure in whom the ambivalence toward history and
revolution is most strongly reflected—the figure of the
father. For revolution is dealt with here in terms of a
profoundly simple metaphor central to both the meaning and action of *Nix's Mate*. The analogue for revolution, for the toppling of authority, is the murder of the
father. The implications a Freudian would see in Fitzvassal's action are obvious but not, I think, nearly as
important to an understanding of the romance as the
political implications of parricide. Political authority,
here, is very noticeably paternal. Edmund Vassal is
both the hero's father and a close friend of the governor. Mr. Wilmer, father of the heroine, is also the

governor's most trusted adviser. In terms of plot Fitzvassal's murder of his father may be contrived and
gratuitous, but it obeys the strictest sort of symbolic
necessity. Revolution is parricide. Even Fitzvassal's
piracy, which operates as a kind of metaphor for his
revolutionary tendencies, has all the sinister connotations of parricide. Edmund Vassal is part owner of the
ship his son seized by mutiny to become a pirate. And
more significantly, Fitzvassal inadvertently kills his
father while committing an act of piracy.[11]

What sort of revolution, one wonders, is *not* associated with the murder of the father? What saves the
successful revolution portrayed in *Nix's Mate* from the
stain of parricide? The answer, quite simply, is that
this revolution is no attack on the fathers because it is
conducted, both symbolically and literally, by the
fathers themselves. This is the patriarchal idea of revolution linked with the figure of the regicide; and *Nix's
Mate* is interesting largely because of the light it sheds
on the nature and the sources of this curious idea.
Thus, in *Nix's Mate*, the "new" government is actually
the "old" charter government, with eighty-six-year-old
Simon Bradstreet at its head. The revolution is led by
an old philosopher named Temple. A final irony is that
while Fitzvassal, who has supported the revolutionary
cause, is sentenced to death by the authority he helped
to establish, Mr. Wilmer, who had been on the side of

[11] The association of piracy with revolution was hardly original
with Dawes. Cooper, for example, had made this association in
The Red Rover (1828). That Dawes had Cooper in mind is suggested by the fact that the pirate ship, in both books, is called the
Dolphin.

the royal governor, is not only forgiven but elected to a magistracy as well. To be sure the patriarchal aspect of this revolution is partly a matter of historical fidelity: Bradstreet, for instance, *was* eighty-six in 1689. But this historical explanation hardly accounts for the emphasis put on the age and previous authority of the revolutionaries. It certainly does not explain the magistracy of Mr. Wilmer.

One explanation for this patriarchal idea of revolution—both in *Nix's Mate* and in the works of many of Dawes's contemporaries—would seem to lie in certain political considerations that had come, by 1839, to influence attitudes toward the American Revolution. The French Revolution, especially as its principles were associated with Jeffersonian Republicanism, represented a threat to Federalists who honored our own "revolutionary" fathers but desired no further change —men for whom the greatest revolutionary hero of all was the Father of His Country. For these Federalists, and later for their Whig successors confronted with "revolutionary" Jacksonian democracy, it was convenient to distinguish between two ideas of revolution— one American and one French. "Especially in New England," writes Wesley Frank Craven, "the reaction against the French Revolution came promptly to lend . . . a new emphasis to the idea that our own Revolution had been fought simply in defense of the 'ancient ground' seized by the liberty-loving first settlers."[12] The American Revolution, unlike French Republican-

[12] Wesley Frank Craven, *The Legend of the Founding Fathers*, p. 60.

ism or Jacksonian democracy, had not been an attack on the *status quo*. It represented, in fact, a *return* to the *status quo*. The American Revolution had restored the "ancient" liberties initially secured by the founding fathers. The Federalist or Whig—that is to say, the conservative—ideal of 1776 saw progress as ending with the Revolution. To a conservative of the earlier nineteenth century (as indeed to a conservative today) the term "spirit of the Revolution" meant not continuing progress but a return to the presumed virtues of a previous generation.

The problem discussed here is a problem encountered by any typological historian when the great antitype in the *future* for the events he is describing is, from his own point in time, in the *past*. How, in political terms, was the historian to treat events after the Revolution—including his own act of writing about that revolution? Or, in terms of the theology which was the source of typological history, how was one to treat the events that followed the great anti-type of Old Testament history, the birth of Christ? In political terms a Bancroft simply continued "progress" past the anti-type (the Revolution) into the present and the future. "Progress" meant, for Bancroft, a continuing revolution. But Bancroft was a Jacksonian Democrat, and most of the writers we are dealing with (Cooper and Hawthorne are significant exceptions) were Whigs. Bancroft's solution was not a possibility for these Whigs, as they were unwilling to follow the logic of "progress" into the present.

They were left with a curiously conservative idea of

revolution. Since they regarded the Revolution of 1776 as the fulfillment of American progress, they were bound to regard any change since that event, not as progress, but as deterioration. Thus John Neal, asking a group of Whigs in 1838 what the Fourth of July should mean to the nineteenth-century present, answered: "Is it not briefly and substantially this, that just in proportion as we have departed from the usages of our fathers—exactly in that proportion have we been afflicted as a people; and that, just in proportion as we have turned back to those usages, just in that proportion has prosperity returned to us, as a people?"[13] One recalls Dawes's lament for the passing of the "old stock"—his comparison of 1689 not with 1776 but with 1839. Neal called, a year before *Nix's Mate*, for a return to the "spirit" of the fathers. In *Nix's Mate* the toppling of Andros restores, not just the "spirit" of the fathers, but the fathers themselves. Bradstreet, for instance, is quite literally a founding father. Thus what begins as a hymn to progress ends as an evocation of the myth of decline, the myth of the founding fathers.

In this context one can see how in the puzzling figure of Fitzvassal Dawes reveals his own sense of extreme frustration in approaching the myth and the stereotype of the founding fathers. Dawes and his generation of American writers (including Hawthorne) came of age at a time when literary and political fashion called for the glorification of the past, yet they were of the present. Glory lay in great deeds, but great deeds were neither needed nor wanted after the Revolution; these writers could only commemorate them. The great

---

[13] John Neal, *Oration, July 4, 1838*, Portland, Me., 1838, p. 24.

men, in an age and land that still refused to take literature seriously as a career, were the fathers; these writers were sons, or grandsons. This sense of frustration shines through many of the works of the period—most notably, as we shall see in Chapter Three, in Hawthorne's "The Custom-House" and even in *The Scarlet Letter*. Thus when Rufus Dawes, himself the grandson of a revolutionary colonel and author of a dedicatory poem to the Bunker Hill monument, has Edward Fitzvassal sentenced to death in the midst of a revolutionary celebration, he is portraying, in a sense, his own predicament. Fitzvassal, unlike the young men of Dawes's generation, is actually present during his revolution. But he is prevented from participating just as effectively as if he were not present; and he is defeated, I would contend, by the same fathers who so oppressed Dawes and his contemporaries. Bradstreet and the other revolutionary leaders are not so much conventional representations as representations of a convention—stereotyped embodiments of a nineteenth-century idea about history. They represent the feeling that a glorious national history has ended before the sons have come of age, so that the sons cannot assert their own importance without challenging the importance of their fathers. The exclusion and ultimate destruction of Fitzvassal make sense only when viewed as an enactment of Dawes's own uneasiness with the conventions arising from conservative "revolutionary" rhetoric.

One would like to know just how aware Dawes was of revealing his uneasiness. One is never quite sure whether or not the destruction of Fitzvassal, with all its Byronic overtones, is meant to be ironic—whether

Dawes means to attack the convention of the fathers or to support it. Is Fitzvassal a young man justly punished for piracy and parricide? Or is he a furious young rebel justly outraged by fate, by his undeserved exclusion from the great affairs of life? Is he, in short, Satan or Manfred? Such founding fathers as Bradstreet are anything but tyrannical agents of an evil destiny. And yet the sympathy with which Fitzvassal is presented will not permit the reader to accept his destruction without questioning the values these founding fathers represent. One even wonders whether the poison-before-pardon device of the ending is meant to absolve the founders of killing the hero or to represent an act of social defiance à la Werther. Suffice it to say that *Nix's Mate* is an extremely confused book. This confusion is interesting for our purposes because it seems to reflect, to grow from, a radical ambivalence on the part of the author toward the stereotyped myth of the founding fathers. Dawes was finally unable to resolve the contradiction between the progressive myth of history recommended by the romantic historians and the myth of decline associated with the figure of the noble patriarch. His failure indicates the complexity of the materials he was dealing with, and the nature of the problems which Hawthorne confronted with so much more success.

Revolution and Independence: Hawthorne's Founders

Hawthorne turned to the New England Puritans, as material for fiction, at the very beginning of his career.

One of his earliest publishing ventures was to have been a collection of stories called *Seven Tales of My Native Land*. The seven stories all dealt with New England, and some, apparently, dealt with the New England past. Most of the stories were probably written during or shortly following Hawthorne's senior year at Bowdoin, 1824-1825. *Seven Tales* never appeared and most of the stories were destroyed, although one of them seems to have survived, in a revised form, in "Alice Doane's Appeal."[14]

In the ten years following his graduation from Bowdoin Hawthorne drew pretty steadily, in his fiction, on the history of the Puritans. Between 1830, when his first published works appeared, and 1837, Hawthorne published nine tales based on seventeenth-century New England history. The last of these, "Endicott and the Red Cross," appeared in the Salem *Gazette* in 1837, after which time Hawthorne abandoned the history of the Puritans, as a topic for fiction, for almost fifteen years.[15] In 1849 he returned to the Puritans, first in the

[14] For a fuller description of *Seven Tales of My Native Land*, see Randall Stewart, *Nathaniel Hawthorne: A Biography*, New Haven, 1948, pp. 24, 29-30.

[15] In 1838 and 1839 Hawthorne extended his fictional portrayal of New England history into the eighteenth century with the four "Legends of the Province House" that appeared separately in the *Democratic Review* and then together in *Twice-Told Tales* (1842). These stories are also related thematically to the tales presently under discussion. I have left them out of the present study (except for brief consideration in the first part of the Epilogue) because, although they are concerned with the New England past, they are not concerned with the seventeenth century, nor with Puritanism. The same reasons have led me, albeit reluctantly, to exclude what is certainly one of Hawthorne's best historical tales, "My Kinsman, Major Molineux."

historical sketch of Salem entitled "Main Street," and then in *The Scarlet Letter*, which was finished and published in 1850. Hawthorne's last fictional treatment of the Puritans occurs in the opening chapter of *The House of the Seven Gables*, describing the historical basis of the feud between the Maules and the Pyncheons.

Hawthorne also turned to the seventeenth-century past in a number of less known more openly "historical" works. Actually "Main Street" falls into this category since it uses a fictional frame—a "showman" exhibiting a panorama of Salem's main street—as a device for relating real historical events. Near the beginning of his career Hawthorne published a few biographical sketches of seventeenth-century New Englanders— most notably, to my mind, "Mrs. Hutchinson," which appeared in the Salem *Gazette* in 1830. And in 1841 Hawthorne published *Grandfather's Chair*, a history of New England for children. In this last work "Grandfather" relates important or picturesque events of New England history that are supposed to have had some connection with the chair in which he now sits. With the exception of "Main Street," these quasi-historical writings are on a decidedly lower level than are Hawthorne's fictional treatments of the New England past. But they can be useful in filling in certain aspects of Hawthorne's attitude toward the Puritans.

In any case, in most of these writings (fiction or history) the figure of the stern and authoritarian noble patriarch is every bit as important as in the writings of Hawthorne's contemporaries, perhaps even more so.

One thinks, for instance, of the description of the procession of magistrates, near the end of *The Scarlet
Letter*—the description of those "primitive statesmen"
who "had fortitude and self-reliance, and, in time of
difficulty or peril, stood up for the welfare of the state
like a line of cliffs against a tempestuous tide" [238].
Such descriptions of the original settlers can be found
in nearly all of Hawthorne's tales in which the original
settlers play a part. For instance, in "Mrs. Hutchinson," one of Hawthorne's first works to be published,
Hawthorne refers to "those blessed fathers of the land,
who rank in our veneration next to the evangelists of
Holy Writ" [223].[16] It is not surprising that Hawthorne joined in the contemporary worship of the image
of John Winthrop, the founding father of Massachusetts. "In the highest place," Hawthorne says, describing the assembled magistrates in "Mrs. Hutchinson,"
"sits Winthrop,—a man by whom the innocent and
guilty might alike desire to be judged; the first confiding in his integrity and wisdom, the latter hoping in
his mildness" [223]. Here, quite clearly, we have the
conventional figure of the founding father.

In one of his early stories, "The Gray Champion,"
Hawthorne draws directly on the body of historical
legend most closely linked to the myth of the founding
fathers—the legend of the regicides. "The Gray Cham-

[16] The rest of this sentence is also important, though not for
our present concerns. "And here, also," Hawthorne continues, "are
many, unpurified from the fiercest errors of the age, and ready to
propagate the religion of peace by violence" [223]. Hawthorne's
treatment of Puritan intolerance, and of the narrow Puritan, is
taken up in Chapter Three.

pion" was first published in the *New England Magazine* in 1835. Two years later it was included in *Twice-
Told Tales* as the opening story, and it retained that
important position in the expanded version of *Twice-
Told Tales* that appeared in 1842. The "plot," if it can
be called that, is quite simple. The scene is set in Boston in 1689, just as the first rumors of the projected
Glorious Revolution are reaching New England. The
story concerns the attempt of Governor Andros, at the
head of an armed and mounted procession of royalists,
to frighten a crowd of restless Puritans into submis-
sion. A "remarkable personage" suddenly appears
"from among the people" [25] to defy the governor
and frighten him into a guarded retreat. Within a day,
we are told, the governor and his supporters had been
imprisoned by the people. As for the "remarkable personage"—whom we know by now to have been a regicide or the spirit of a regicide—we learn that he appeared again at the Boston Massacre, at the battle of
Lexington, and the night before the battle of Bunker
Hill. He is, we are told, "the type of New England's
hereditary spirit," the foe to all forms of "tyranny"
[31].

Ten years after Hawthorne, William H. Herbert, in
The Fair Puritan, also saw the symbolic ties between
the legend of the regicide and the Revolution of 1689.[17]

[17] In Herbert's novel—published in three parts in 1844 and
1845—the action culminates in Boston during the Revolution of
1689, where the heroine, granddaughter of the regicide Whalley,
is imprisoned by the corrupt Governor "Andross"—here a Catholic—who is trying to rape or seduce the heroine, and whose name
is misspelled throughout. The book is a fascinating mélange of

But Hawthorne's tale clearly reveals its author's superior talents in the adaptation of historical material for fiction. First, his use of legend—of a spectral rather than a literal regicide—not only lends an appropriate air of mystery to what is after all a symbolic tale, it also saves Hawthorne from the anachronism of placing a palpable regicide in Boston as late as 1689. A more important insight into Hawthorne's art comes with the realization that "The Gray Champion" combines, in one brief action, both the traditional and the symbolic aspects of the conventional regicide. This tale of a regicide rallying a crowd of people is clearly (if loosely) based on the tradition of the Hadley Indian attack, a tradition in itself unrelated to the symbolic function of king-defier. But by changing the Indian attack into an attempted assertion of royal "tyranny," Hawthorne fuses tradition and symbol into a single concise legend.[18]

The meaning of this legend would appear to be

---

conventional cliché and historical ignorance. I will have frequent occasion to refer to it in the ensuing chapters.

[18] Hawthorne displayed his interest in the regicides, and his willingness to be as skeptical as Twain about historical "monuments," in an 1828 visit to Horace Conolly, then a student in New Haven. Conolly reported, so Randall Stewart writes, "their visit to the graves of the regicide judges, in whom Hawthorne was particularly interested, and Hawthorne's disappointment in the Judges' Cave, which he went out to West Rock to see at a cost of $3.50 for hack hire. He called the cave, Conolly said, 'the damndest humbug in America,' adding that 'there was not even a hole in the ground deep enough to bury a dead cat.'" (*Nathaniel Hawthorne*, p. 41.) Hawthorne also treats the 1689 revolution (without regicide) in *Grandfather's Chair* and (very briefly) in the biographical sketch of "Dr. Bullivant" (1831).

abundantly clear: "The Gray Champion" records an early assertion of the revolutionary spirit of New England; it records a type of the American Revolution against England. This is the standard reading of "The Gray Champion" as it was, for romantic historians, the standard reading of the Revolution of 1689.[19] There are elements within the story, however, which seem to conflict with such a reading. For one thing there are some hints of Puritan intolerance in the supposedly "revolutionary" crowd—hints which seem totally unrelated to the story's typological meaning. We learn that the crowd includes "veterans of King Philip's war, who had burned villages and slaughtered young and old, with pious fierceness, while the godly souls through-

[19] This was George Bancroft's interpretation of the incident (see above, p. 34). It is even possible that Hawthorne was influenced by Bancroft, although such influence would be extremely difficult to prove. Bancroft's first volume (containing his account of the 1689 revolution) appeared in 1834, a year before "The Gray Champion" was published. But "The Gray Champion" was given to the publisher in 1834 (see Stewart, *Nathaniel Hawthorne*, p. 32), so the timing would have to have been very close. It cannot be shown that Hawthorne read Bancroft before 1837, when he withdrew the first volume of the *History* from the Salem Athenaeum library (see Marion L. Kesselring, *Hawthorne's Reading, 1828-1850*, New York, 1949, p. 44). But it is almost unbelievable that Hawthorne would not have devoured Bancroft's volume as soon as it appeared. "Grandfather," in *Grandfather's Chair*, heartily recommends "Mr. Bancroft's History" to the most serious of his young auditors [456]. Bancroft is also mentioned favorably in "The Old Manse" [13]. In any case, the question of whether or not Bancroft actually influenced "The Gray Champion" is relatively unimportant. What matters is that Hawthorne, like Bancroft, expressed the conventional typological view of the Revolution of 1689.

out the land were helping them with prayer" [23]. But there is hardly enough of this sort of thing seriously to interfere with the story's revolutionary atmosphere.

A more important problem appears to be raised by the age and authoritarian demeanor of the main characters of "The Gray Champion." "There were men in the street that day," we are told, "who had worshipped there beneath the trees, before a house was reared to the God for whom they had become exiles" [23]. Bradstreet, "a patriarch of nearly ninety" [24], is literally a founding father. The champion himself, the revolutionary regicide, is an "ancient man," wearing the "old Puritan dress," recognized by the "fathers of the people, those of fourscore years and upwards" [26-27]. We are not long in recognizing the features of the conventional regicide in this "hoary sire, the relic of long-departed times," characterized by "the eye, the face, and attitude of command" [27-28].[20]

To a modern reader, for whom "revolution" is almost necessarily associated with youth, the age and authority of such a character seem seriously to compromise the revolutionary meaning of "The Gray Champion." The age of the Champion has led at least one critic into an ironic reading of the story—an assertion that beneath its overtly patriotic or democratic surface, the story is designed to subvert the whole idea of patriot-

[20] In the treatment of the 1689 revolution in *Grandfather's Chair*, the great age of Bradstreet is repeatedly emphasized. Indeed it seems, to "Grandfather," altogether the most important feature of the revolution [481-83].

ism by revealing it to be the self-justifying propaganda of authority-figures.[21] This is a tempting reading, particularly in view of the current alliance of conservative ideology and so-called "revolutionary" rhetoric (the title "Daughters of the American Revolution" is a case in point). But such an ironic reading of "The Gray Champion" ignores the meaning of "revolution" for Hawthorne and his contemporaries. Such a reading assumes that "revolution" must be "democratic," and that therefore all fathers and father-figures are authoritarian and thus "anti-revolutionary." This may be true in our own age. But Hawthorne lived and wrote in an age which thought of its greatest "revolutionary" hero as the Father of his Country, and "The Gray Champion" is very much a product of this age. It is not an ironic attack on the conservative ideal of the Revolution. It is, on the contrary, a sincere expression of that ideal through a character conventionally associated with that ideal in the fiction of Hawthorne's contemporaries—the figure of the founding father as regicide. The Champion is the "type" not of the future but of the past, not of 1776 but of "New England's *hereditary* spirit" [31, italics mine]. This "spirit" has its harsh side, as the veterans of King Philip's War suggest. But the emphasis here is on nobility. Hawthorne does not confuse the spirit of New England and the Revolution with the spirit of democratic equality; but the spirit is no less noble for that. When the Champion emerges "from among the people" [25], Hawthorne does not

[21] See Frederick Crews, *The Sins of the Fathers: Hawthorne's Psychological Themes*, New York, 1966, pp. 39-41.

mean that the Champion typifies or pretends to typify any notion of democratic equality. He means, rather, that there is a little of his testy self-reliance in all New Englanders, and that this self-reliance emerges when outsiders threaten to reduce New Englanders to subordination. This "liberty," in Hawthorne's typological reading of seventeenth-century history, is not egalitarianism but independence.

THIS MEANING OF "liberty" should be kept in mind in reading Hawthorne's other clearly typological tale of the Puritans, "Endicott and the Red Cross," which is much more easily read as an ironic attack on supposedly "revolutionary" rhetoric. "Endicott and the Red Cross," which first appeared in the Salem *Gazette* in 1837, is based on an actual event that occurred in Salem in 1634. Apparently under the urging of Roger Williams—whose subsequent banishment to Plymouth was partly a result of the affair—Endicott cut the red cross, which he took to be a sign of "popish idolatry," from the British banner used by the Salem militia.[22] Hawthorne places this material within a clearly typological framework. In the story Endicott's gesture re-

22 Surprisingly enough, this incident is not mentioned by Bancroft, who would have had little enough trouble fitting it into his version of New England history. Hawthorne could have found the incident in Hutchinson's *History of Massachusetts Bay*. Hawthorne also treats the incident in *Grandfather's Chair* [445-48], where he appears to be following Hutchinson rather closely. (For the relation between Hutchinson's *History* and *Grandfather's Chair*, see Edward Dawson, *Hawthorne's Knowledge and Use of New England History: A Study of Sources*, Nashville, Tenn., 1939, pp. 9-10.)

sults, not from the advice of Williams, but in reaction to rumors that Charles I is contemplating "tyrannically violent" measures against the colony. Endicott reacts to these rumors with an impassioned defense of American "liberty." "What have we to do with this mitred prelate," he shouts to a crowd of Puritans, "—with this crowned king? What have we to do with England?" [493]. It is with these words that he cuts the cross from the tricolor banner of England. The people approve heartily,[23] and so, apparently, does Hawthorne, who proceeds to draw the proper typological "moral." "Forever honored," he concludes, "be the name of Endicott! We look back through the mist of ages, and recognize in the rending of the Red Cross from New England's banner the first omen of that deliverance which our fathers consummated after the bones of the stern Puritan had lain more than a century in the dust" [493-94]. Endicott's violent action prefigures the American Revolution.

The problem with "Endicott and the Red Cross" is that this "revolutionary" conclusion hardly seems to follow from the opening description of the scene at Salem. The first few pages of the tale, describing the scene as reflected in the shining armor of Endicott's breastplate, seem meant to convey the suppression, rather than the assertion, of liberty in America. There is a bloody wolf's head nailed to the door of the meet-

[23] Hutchinson, however, notes that "many of the militia refused to train with the mangled, defaced colours." (*History of Massachusetts Bay*, I, 41n.) Hawthorne was apparently willing to stretch the record (if Hutchinson *was* his source, as seems likely) in order to give the act of defiance a popular character.

ing house, while the building itself is surrounded by the tokens of persecution—whipping post, pillory, and stocks. In the last two we see "an Episcopalian and suspected Catholic" and "a fellow-criminal, who had boisterously quaffed a health to the king" [486]. A "Wanton Gospeller," so labeled by a sign on his breast, stands on the steps, and the crowd below is filled with past victims of persecution—men and women with cropped ears, branded cheeks, slit and seared nostrils, and the like. This catalogue of misery is concluded by the description of "a young woman, with no mean share of beauty, whose doom it was to wear the letter A on the breast of her gown, in the eyes of all the world and her own children." "Sporting with her infamy," writes Hawthorne, "the lost and desperate creature had embroidered the fatal token in scarlet cloth, with golden thread and the nicest art of needlework; so that the capital A might have been thought to mean Admirable, or anything rather than Adulteress" [487].

The emphasis of the story shifts when Roger Williams arrives with the news of the king's supposed designs on New England. Even here, however, the attack on Puritan intolerance surfaces occasionally. Thus when the patriotically aroused Endicott tells the crowd that they came to New England "for the enjoyment of our civil rights," "for liberty to worship God according to our conscience," the Wanton Gospeller interrupts to demand, "Call you this liberty of conscience?" We are told that at this point "a sad and quiet smile flitted across the mild visage of Roger Williams" [491]. The future outcast is apparently identifying with the present prisoner. There would appear to be an enormous contradiction here between Endicott's assertion of liberty from England, and his suppression of the liberty of others. The contradiction looms so large, since intolerance receives so much emphasis, that one is even more tempted than in "The Gray Champion" to advance an ironic reading. The emphasis on intolerance, one feels, can only be meant to undercut Endicott's spurious "revolutionary" rhetoric about "liberty."

Hawthorne's handling of intolerance is more properly the concern of Chapter Three than of the present chapter; but it is important to note here, with respect to "Endicott and the Red Cross," that the apparent contradiction between intolerance and nobility can be misunderstood. It is there, to be sure. But it presents less of a problem if Endicott is seen, as he should be seen, in relation to the conventional figure of the noble founder—the figure also embodied in the Gray Champion. For like the "liberty" of the Champion, Endicott's "liberty" has to do with independence rather than democracy. The point of the irony is not that Endicott's intolerance undercuts his independence, but that the two qualities are inextricably joined in a single representative individual. Hawthorne embodies in the character of Endicott a sense that the nobility and narrowness of the founding fathers are not necessarily distinct and separable characteristics. The intransigent severity that enabled the Puritans to summon enough courage to defy England also led them to persecute their neighbors. The expense of courage was intolerance. If the mild Williams is later to be exiled (although this fact is not mentioned in the story), it is also worth noting that the mild Williams specifically counsels against standing up to England.[24]

A better way of putting all this is to say that an ethical judgment for or against Puritanism is not really the point of "Endicott and the Red Cross." Insofar as the method of the story is ironic, it is the function of the irony not to undercut Endicott's claims to virtue but to make the portrayal of him—and of what he represents—as historically objective as possible. For the subject of the story is profoundly historical. "Endicott and the Red Cross" records the symbolic birth of the American character—as "The Gray Champion" records a resurgence of that character. The tale portrays one

[24] The use of Williams is one of the more curious features of "Endicott and the Red Cross," and Hawthorne's portrayal of Williams here represents a major departure from Williams's role in Hutchinson's *History* and in *Grandfather's Chair*. Williams is fully implicated in Endicott's action in the *History* and in *Grandfather's Chair*. "Were it my business to draw a sword," says Williams to Endicott in *Grandfather's Chair*, "I should reckon it sinful to fight under such a banner" [446]. Yet in the tale, Endicott's action is the result of rumors contained in Winthrop's letter, and Williams strongly opposes cutting the cross from the flag.

In general Hawthorne's changes (in the story) have the effect of moving Williams into opposition to Endicott's authoritarian regime—an opposition also suggested by Williams's "sad smile" at the words of the Wanton Gospeller. Yet Hawthorne very curiously never mentions the fact that Williams will soon be banished for this opposition; Williams here, for all his mildness, is an accepted member of the community. Even more curiously, Hawthorne violates historical accuracy in order to associate Williams, in age, with the patriarchal Puritan establishment. Hawthorne describes Williams, who would have been in his middle thirties at the time of the story, as "an elderly gentleman" [488].

of the first moments when Americans defined themselves as distinct from the people they left behind in England. On the one hand Hawthorne glories in Endicott's deed as a heroic act of self-definition. On the other hand, however, he is aware too that something was lost through Endicott's heroism. Endicott repudiates England, and to the extent that England represents external tyranny it is well lost. But the loss of England involves as well the loss of certain kinds of passion, gaiety, and humor. The royalist incarcerated for having "boisterously quaffed a health to the king" [486] is hardly a tyrant. The woman with the scarlet A is important not only because she foreshadows Hester Prynne, but also because her punishment indicates the fate of sensual beauty in the New World. It is significant that the badge of her shame is the same color as the cross that Endicott rips from the British flag. Perhaps this is the point of the mild Roger Williams: not that he is now an outsider (he is not), but that he will soon inevitably become one.

Thus what matters in "Endicott and the Red Cross" and "The Gray Champion" is not that "liberty of conscience" is compromised by intolerance, although Hawthorne is aware that it is compromised. Hawthorne is willing to accept this intolerance as a necessary concomitant to the heroic act of self-definition in separating from England. What matters in these stories, especially in "Endicott and the Red Cross," is that the violence of separation, necessitated by the particular historical situation in which it takes places, causes the American character to be established on narrow lines—

{}

through an act of exclusion rather than through absorption. What matters to Hawthorne is not his own personal opinion of intolerance, but what he thinks have been the results of intolerance—its effects on the formation of the American character.[25] Endicott, in this story, is faced with a choice between England and America, old and new. He chooses the new, and the point of the story is that he is choosing for all America, for the future as well as for the present.[26] In Endicott's action the American character takes in, along with all the heroism and self-reliance that Hawthorne so admires, a certain narrowness of sensibility. Endicott, in Haw-

[25] In a larger (less specifically historical) sense, Endicott is another example in Hawthorne's fiction (Aylmer and especially Hollingsworth are others) of the general ethical proposition that obsession with schemes of reform (whether alchemy, prison reform, or Puritanism) leads eventually to an inhuman narrowness of self-definition on the part of the reformer. Obsession, that is to say, leads to a loss of "human sympathy." In focusing here on the *historical* significance of Endicott, I do not mean to deny by implication his more general *ethical* significance for Hawthorne. My point here is that if America is to be regarded as the result of an aborted scheme of reform (Puritanism), then perhaps the historical corollary to the general proposition becomes at least as important as the proposition itself. In any case it should hardly be surprising that Hawthorne's historical ideas are related to his more general ideas about human behavior. If I stress the former at the expense of the latter it is only to redress the balance of most previous Hawthorne criticism.

[26] Compare Mrs. Q. D. Leavis's comment on Hawthorne's historical fiction: "As I see it," she writes, "Hawthorne's sense of being a part of the contemporary America could be expressed only in concern for its evolution—he needed to see how it had come about, and by discovering what America had, culturally speaking, started from and with, to find out what choices faced his countrymen." ("Hawthorne as Poet," in A. N. Kaul [ed.], *Hawthorne* [Twentieth Century Views], Englewood Cliffs, N.J., 1966, p. 28.)

thorne's story, is ultimately intended as an archetypal American—representing the beginnings of a separate American identity in the New World. And in creating this archetypal figure of the American, Hawthorne drew heavily on the dominant conventional character in the historical romance of New England, the figure of the stern but noble founding father.

Fathers and Sons: The Myth of Decline

The characterization of the founding fathers as noble patriarchs is associated, in the fiction of Hawthorne's contemporaries, with the myth of historical decline from the days of those founders. Cooper portrays such decline in *The Wept of Wish-Ton-Wish*. And although Cooper perhaps insists on decline more than most of his contemporaries, he is by no means alone in his general feeling that the second and third generations of Puritans were no match for their fathers or grandfathers. As Eliza Buckminster Lee puts it at the beginning of *Naomi*: the "first settlers brought with them the genial influences, the refining culture, of a high state of civilization. The next generation were sterner and harsher men" [4].

We should not be surprised, considering the importance of the noble patriarch in Hawthorne's fiction, to find that Hawthorne, too, sees a rapid and marked decline from the manliness of the first generation of Puritans. For instance, describing the crowd and the "old spirit" of the founders at the beginning of "The Gray Champion," Hawthorne comments ominously:

"Indeed, it was not yet time for the old spirit to be extinct; since there were men in the street that day who had worshipped there beneath the trees, before a house was reared to the God for whom they had become exiles" [23]. The implication is that the "old spirit" of the founders survives only in the breasts of those founders themselves, now a group of superannuated old men. In the sons and grandsons, it would seem, such "spirit" is sadly lacking. Hawthorne was willing to accept the narrow intolerance of an Endicott as the necessary price of his stern and rugged manly courage. But should the courage be lost to succeeding generations, what then would remain? One answer to this question can be seen in the description of Endicott in 1659, as leader of the Quaker persecutions, in "The Gentle Boy." "He was a man," we are told, "of narrow mind and imperfect education, and his uncompromising bigotry was made hot and mischievous by violent and hasty passions; he exerted his influence indecorously and unjustifiably to compass the death of the enthusiasts; and his whole conduct, in respect to them, was marked by brutal cruelty" [86]. In this story even the noble Endicott of the 1620's has become *merely* intolerant. Furthermore there are strong suggestions in "The Gentle Boy" that the intolerance of the Puritans increased in succeeding generations. As Tobias Pearson and his wife take a little Quaker boy to the Puritan meeting house their way is blocked by a hostile "phalanx" of neighbors. This "phalanx" includes, we are told, "several of the oldest members of the congregation, many of the middle aged, and nearly all the younger males" [96].[27]

Hawthorne's fullest description of this process of decline occurs in the historical sketch "Main Street." Here, as is usual in Hawthorne's fiction, the first generation of Puritans is presented as possessing, for all its austerity, redeeming qualities of nobility and manhood. "Their house of worship," says the narrator of the first settlers, "like their ceremonial, was naked, simple, and severe. But the zeal of a recovered faith burned like a lamp within their hearts, enriching every-

[27] For that matter, modern historians of New England still see a narrowing in the scope and nature of Puritanism between 1630 and 1700. For example, Perry Miller contends in "Errand into the Wilderness" that American Puritanism changed as the New England settlers began to regard what had been means toward the larger purposes of the migration as the ends of the migration. Their errand lost the sense of universal meaning which had been part of it when the *Arbella* set sail in 1630. From our point of view it is interesting that Professor Miller sees this loss as being underscored by the passing of the first generation, regarded even by their sons as noble founding fathers. "This sense of the meaning having gone out of life," he writes, "that all adventures are over, that no great days and no heroism lie ahead, is particularly galling when it falls upon a son whose father once was the public hero." (*Errand into the Wilderness*, New York, 1956, p. 14.) It is interesting to note how "modern"—allowing for differences of conceptual vocabulary—Hawthorne's treatment of the Puritans can be. (On this point compare David Levin, "Hawthorne's Romances: The Value of Puritan History," in *In Defense of Historical Literature*, New York, 1967, pp. 103-104.)

One might also compare Roy R. Male's description of Hawthorne's version of New England history. "With the passing of the first generation," he writes, "religious gloom was maintained with only a counterfeit of the earlier religious ardor. . . . The solid piety of the early Puritans was transmuted into neurotic persecutions of Quakers and witches." (*Hawthorne's Tragic Vision*, New York, 1957, p. 40.)

thing around them with its radiance." "All was well," the narrator continues, "so long as their lamps were freshly kindled at the heavenly flame. After a while, however, whether in their time or their children's, these lamps began to burn more dimly, or with a less genuine lustre; and then it might be seen how hard, cold, and confined was their system,—how like an iron cage was that which they called Liberty" [449]. If Hawthorne's version of Puritan history is unique for its time, it is not unique because it asserts decline from father to son, but rather because Hawthorne analyzes and attempts to understand this decline. In this respect a long passage from "Main Street" deserves extended quotation:

. . . when the first novelty and stir of spirit had subsided [Hawthorne writes]—when the new settlement, between the forest-border and the sea, had become actually a little town,—its daily life must have trudged onward with hardly anything to diversify and enliven it, while also its rigidity could not fail to cause miserable distortions of the moral nature. Such a life was sinister to the intellect, and sinister to the heart; especially when one generation had bequeathed its religious gloom, and the counterfeit of its religious ardor, to the next; for these characteristics, as was inevitable, assumed the form both of hypocrisy and exaggeration, by being inherited from the example and precept of other human beings, and not from an original and spiritual source. The sons and grandchildren of the first settlers were a race of lower and narrower souls than their progenitors had been. The latter were stern, severe, intolerant, but not superstitious, not even fanatical; and endowed, if any men of that age were, with a far-seeing worldly sagacity. But it was impossible for the succeeding race to grow up, in heaven's freedom, beneath the discipline which their gloomy energy of character had established. . . . [459-60]

If any of Hawthorne's Puritans resemble the "Puritans" attacked as symbols of repression by Mencken and his contemporaries, they are not the founders but their descendants—"the sons and grandchildren of the first settlers." The story which most overtly and penetratingly probes the mentality of these "sons and grandchildren" is no doubt "Young Goodman Brown." Three lesser treatments of the same mentality are "The Man of Adamant," "The Minister's Black Veil" and "Alice Doane's Appeal."

Both "The Minister's Black Veil" and "The Man of Adamant" deal with men who, on the basis of an abstract religious principle, cut themselves off from communion with mankind.[28] In both stories the self-

[28] Neither of these stories is "historical" in the sense that "The Gray Champion" and "Endicott and the Red Cross" are "historical"—that is to say, neither of these stories deals with an important, recorded past event. One of the stories is, however, based on a real person. "The Minister's Black Veil," as Hawthorne himself notes at the outset of the story, is based on the career of Joseph Moody of York, Maine, a minister who began wearing a veil after accidentally killing his best friend. But Hawthorne is by no means concerned with reproducing the details of Moody's life: for instance, while Hooper's bachelorhood is important to the story, Moody took a wife at the age of thirty-three. (See Dawson, *Hawthorne's Knowledge and Use of New England History*, p. 26.) "The Man of Adamant," not surprisingly, is not based on any real person. Rather it would appear to have grown out of two 1835 notebook entries (which also anticipate "Ethan Brand"): "The story of a man, cold and hard-hearted, and acknowledging no brotherhood with mankind. . . ." "It might be stated, as the closing circumstance of a tale, that the body of one of the characters had

willed isolation of the hero is embodied in his repudiation of the love and sympathy of a virtuous and beautiful woman. In "The Man of Adamant" Richard Digby,
"the gloomiest and most intolerant of a stern brotherhood" [564], decides that his faith is the only true faith,
that he alone is fit for salvation, and thereby determines
to flee mankind for the wilderness. There he hides himself in a secluded cave. Three days later the ghost of
a young woman named Mary Goffe[29] appears to warn
him that the waters of the cave are dangerous to him.
She asks him instead to drink fresh spring water and
to return to humanity. He refuses, and at the moment
of refusal his heart (owing, we are assured, to the
waters of the cave and to a peculiar coronary disease)
stops beating and turns to stone. Eventually Digby's
entire body turns to calcium, in which form it is dis-
covered 100 years later.

"The Minister's Black Veil," although it was published one year *before* "The Man of Adamant," is by
far the more complex of the two stories. It tells of a
mild-mannered bachelor, Parson Hooper, who one day
appears before his congregation wearing a black veil
over his features—a veil he insists on wearing even to
the grave. It is clear that Hooper means the veil as
some sort of symbol of "secret sin," but it is not at all
clear what Hawthorne means by the veil, or by Hoop-

---

been petrified, and still existed in that state." (*Passages from the
American Notebooks*, p. 24.) Both stories first appeared in the
Token—"The Minister's Black Veil" in 1836 and "The Man of
Adamant" in 1837.

[29] In spite of her name this girl is not connected, in the story,
with the regicide Goffe.

er's story. On the one hand we may find Hooper guilty of spiritual pride, and therefore fully deserving of the increasing isolation that results from wearing the veil. On the other hand we may accept his assumption of the veil as sincere and admirable, and therefore censure the townspeople for unfeelingly rejecting him. The difficulty of the story is clearest in the scene in which the engagement between Hooper and a woman named Elizabeth is broken off. "Lift the veil but once," she asks, "and look me in the face" [63]. Hooper refuses, and Elizabeth bids him farewell. Are we to take Hooper as a more subdued Richard Digby, rejecting human sympathy for a religious ideal; or are we to see Hooper as justified and *Elizabeth*, therefore, as wanting in sympathy? One may look ahead to Hawthorne's announced determination, at the beginning of "The Custom-House," to "keep the inmost Me behind its veil" [4], or to Zenobia's legend of "The Silvery Veil" in *The Blithedale Romance*, in which Theodore proves himself unworthy of the Veiled Lady by insisting that she remove her veil before he gives her his love. Yet Elizabeth is no Theodore. She is sincere and loving, and we learn at the close that she remains faithful to Hooper to the end. And Hooper seems to do more than simply accept separation from Elizabeth and mankind; he seems positively to desire such separation. "This dismal shade," he shouts almost gleefully to Elizabeth, "must separate me from the world: even you, Elizabeth, can never come behind it!" [62].

In assuming the black veil Hooper appears to be motivated by a perception of the general sinfulness of man with which Hawthorne, the reader feels, would undoubtedly agree. But the action which Hooper takes on the basis of his perception of sin serves only, ironically, to compound that sin. Hooper preaches his first sermon after assuming the veil on "secret sin, and those sad mysteries which we hide from our nearest and dearest, and would fain conceal from our own consciousness, even forgetting that the Omniscient can detect them" [55]. Yet it is surely ironic that one concerned with overcoming concealment should conceal himself. "When the friend shows his inmost heart to his friend," declares Hooper on his deathbed; "the lover to his best beloved; when man does not vainly shrink from the eye of his Creator, loathsomely treasuring up the secret of his sin; then deem me a monster, for the symbol beneath which I have lived, and die! I look around me, and, lo! on every visage a Black Veil!" [69]. Yet by assuming the veil Hooper himself has become a sinner, perhaps the greatest sinner of them all. The veil, we are told, "had separated him from cheerful brotherhood and woman's love, and kept him in that saddest of all prisons, his own heart" [67]. Having placed a veil between himself and the world Hooper comes to attribute the veil's blackness to the world itself. The veil, we are told, "probably did not intercept his sight, further than to give a darkened aspect to all living and inanimate things" [53]. Hooper recoils from a world in which he can see only evil; but this is an evil he has projected from himself into that world.

"The Man of Adamant" and "The Minister's Black

Veil" criticize the Puritans, not for seeing sin in the world, but for seeing nothing else. The first settlers of New England, Hawthorne wrote in "Main Street," "were endowed . . . with a far-seeing worldly sagacity" [460]. For all their intolerance they were men of this world. In Digby and Hooper intolerance has become superstition. They flee a world tarnished by their own imaginations. Of course the notion of projected evil is not, in these stories, located specifically in the latter half of the seventeenth century.[30] Nonetheless Hawthorne frequently does associate the mentality of a Digby or a Hooper with the second and third generations in New England. Hooper, for instance, foreshadows Arthur Dimmesdale—both men conceal a secret sin, and both are made better preachers by the act of concealment. One can see the traits of Digby and Hooper in Young Goodman Brown. And such traits are associated with the third generation of New England Puritans in one of Hawthorne's earliest extant stories, "Alice Doane's Appeal."

"Alice Doane's Appeal" consists of a number of loosely related fragments rather than a coherent narrative. The

[30] Since Digby has migrated from England, where he had been a more tolerant man and minister, it is possible that the story is meant to take place at the time of the first migration. There is nothing in the tale by which to assign it a more specific date. A reference in "The Minister's Black Veil" to "Governor Belcher's administration" [65], which extended from 1730 to 1741, would place this story in the first half of the eighteenth century. When Hooper assumes the veil he is "about thirty" [53]. Joseph Moody was thirty in 1731. (See Dawson, *Hawthorne's Knowledge and Use of New England History*, p. 27.)

three main fragments are the nineteenth-century frame in which the author escorts two young ladies to Gallows Hill outside Salem, the highly sensational story he tells about Leonard Doane, and a closing evocation of the horror of the Salem witch trials. The story begins with the author's decision to read to his companions a tale he wrote, so he informs us, some years before.[31] The inset tale, which takes place around 1692, begins with the discovery of the body of one Walter Brome on the road between Boston and Salem. We are then abruptly introduced to three characters: Leonard Doane, a young man "characterized by a diseased imagination and morbid feelings"; his "beautiful and virtuous" sister, Alice; and, finally, an evil wizard [284]. Leonard and Alice, we learn, were orphaned when their father was killed in an Indian attack. In an interview with the wizard Leonard confesses that he was jealous of Alice's suspected love for Walter who, it appears, is Leonard's exact counterpart. Leonard tells the wizard that he slew Walter when, in a chance meeting, Walter proved the

[31] The author's description of this "manuscript" as having been one of two in "kinder custody" when he burned the rest of a "series written years ago" [282], combined with other testimony, makes it fairly certain that at least some earlier form of "Alice Doane's Appeal," presumably without the frame, was one of the *Seven Tales of My Native Land*, a series never published but perhaps written as early as Hawthorne's final year at Bowdoin (see above, p. 45). It is not known when the frame, or the final account of the Salem procession, were added. Some version of the story was submitted to the *Token* in 1830, but it did not appear until the final version was published in the *Token* for 1835. No one knows whether the revision took place before or after 1830, or whether, perhaps, there were two revisions. Hawthorne never collected the story, nor does he ever seem to have acknowledged it as his own (his stories in the *Token* were published anonymously).

"shame" of Alice—presumably that she had given in to Walter's advances. Leonard adds a chilling touch to his narrative by relating that, as he looked at the face of his dead victim, a strange transformation seemed to take place. "Methought," he says, "I stood a weeping infant by my father's hearth; by the cold and blood-stained hearth where he lay dead" [287].

After another awkward transition we accompany Leonard and Alice to the Salem graveyard. Leonard is vacillating frantically between belief in his sister's purity and conviction of her corruption. The graves open to release the shapes of all the old settlers of Salem—some of them really "souls accursed" and others "fiends counterfeiting the likeness of departed saints" [290]. To this throng of spirits it is announced that the wizard has controlled the events leading to the murder of Walter, and that Walter was in fact Leonard's twin brother. "The story concluded," announces the author, substituting summary for the words of his manuscript, "with the Appeal of Alice to the spectre of Walter Brome; his reply, absolving her from every stain; and the trembling awe with which ghost and devil fled, as from the sinless presence of an angel" [292].

We return to the nineteenth-century present. As the author tries for one last grisly effect he overreaches himself and the girls begin to laugh at him. As a kind of vengeance he calls up a scene more directly related to the events of 1692 in Salem—a procession of accused "witches" followed by their accusers. The latter are marshaled by the villainous figure of Cotton Mather on horseback, "the one blood-thirsty man, in whom were concentrated those vices of spirit and errors of opinion that sufficed to madden the whole surrounding multitude" [294]. The girls, in terror, compel the author to stop. But the author is satisfied; he has reduced the girls to tears. "The past," he comments, "had done all it could" [294].

This tale has not generally been taken seriously even by Hawthorne's admirers.[32] It has received considerable attention, however, from psychoanalytic critics who see, beneath the chaotic and melodramatic surface, a fictional embodiment of a classical Oedipal situation.[33] In slaying Walter, according to this psychoanalytic reading, Leonard is slaying both his father and the personification of his own wish to commit incest with his sister. There is a good deal of value in such an approach to "Alice Doane's Appeal"; and in fact such an approach seems indispensable to a full understanding of what Hawthorne is doing. But for all its value the reading explains only one part of the story, the inset tale about Leonard Doane. Even if one feels that Leonard's tale is simply an embodiment of a classical Oedipal situation, one must deal with the larger question of the interrelation of the various parts of the story. What, we must ask, since our particular concern is with Hawthorne's historical themes, do Leonard's

[32] Mark Van Doren, for example, dismisses it as a rather superficial mixture of history and Gothic, "a confused rewriting of something done more simply before, perhaps in college." (*Nathaniel Hawthorne*, New York, 1949, p. 72.)

[33] See, for example, Frederick Crews's chapter on "Alice Doane's Appeal" in *The Sins of the Fathers*.

psychological problems have to do with the historical period in which the tale is set? What, more particularly, does the tale of Leonard, Walter, and Alice have to do with the final procession of accused "witches" and accusers—with the Gothic picture of Cotton Mather as superstitious villain? According to one critic, Cotton Mather is, like Leonard's father, simply another villainous father-figure.[34] But there is little justification for such an assertion. There is no indication whatever that Leonard's father was villainous or tyrannical; nor is there any suggestion that Cotton Mather (who was twenty-nine in 1692) is in any sense paternal.

It would seem, rather, that if there is a link between Leonard Doane and Cotton Mather it is to be found in the closest thing to "witchcraft" in Leonard's story, the central graveyard scene in which Leonard and Alice confront the specters or impersonations of the dead of Salem. For one thing this scene shows us what is generally true in Hawthorne's treatment of the New England past, that the first settlers were nobler than their children. Leonard is a far cry from these "early settlers, those old illustrious ones, the heroes of tradition and fireside legends, the men of history." We see the "venerable shapes" of old pastors, and the specters of those who "were old defenders of the infant colony, and gleamed forth in their steel-caps and bright breast-plates, as if starting up at an Indian war-cry" [290]. It may be objected that the nobility of these founders is illusory, that they immediately become part of a scene so filled with evil that it seems "as if the unimagi-

<hr>

[34] *Ibid.*, p. 57.

nable sin of twenty worlds were collected there" [291]. There are two points to be made to counter this objection. First, the transformation of the shapes of pious founders into fiends is no argument the founders themselves were primarily evil. For this "vision" consists not of the founders themselves but only of the sinful founders mixed with "false spectres of good men" [291].[35] A second, more significant point is the fact that the transformation of the fathers from pious exemplars into devils seems to be a reflection, not so much of the actual condition of the founders, as of Leonard's "diseased imagination and morbid feelings." I am not arguing that Hawthorne thought the founders of New England (or anyone, for that matter) to be without sin. But Leonard's graveyard vision is horribly distorted and exaggerated. All the examples of sin, so overtly sexual, are notable for their lack of basis in fact. Virgins, even though their virginity is not denied, wear looks of lechery. Lovers who lamented the early

[35] Hyatt Waggoner minimizes the importance of this qualification, which he sees as contradicting or rationalizing the "true" meaning of the ghosts—namely, that *all* the dead seem to be damned. (*Hawthorne: A Critical Study*, Cambridge, Mass., 1963, pp. 54-55.) Hawthorne's distinction is neither contrived nor trivial however. In fact it was to a large extent the failure of the judges to observe this distinction between people and "specters" impersonating them that led to the unjust convictions for witchcraft in 1692. The same distinction lies behind Hamlet's uncertainty about his father's ghost:

> . . . The spirit that I have seen
> May be a devil, and the devil hath power
> T'assume a pleasing shape. . . . (ii, ii, 584-86)

In any case, since Hawthorne makes this distinction twice within two pages, I assume it is safe to say that he means it.

deaths of those they loved, and whose earthly purity does not seem to be in question, now leer at each other with hatred and scorn. Most revealing, when one considers Leonard's vacillation between belief in his sister's purity and horror at her guilt, is the description of "the features of those who had passed from a holy life to heaven" which, we are told, "would vary to and fro, between their assumed aspect and the fiendish lineaments whence they had been transformed" [291]. This apparition of worldly evil, while it may begin in a genuine awareness of real sin, ends as a grotesque product of Leonard's diseased state of mind.

In this sense Leonard's vision is analogous to the "Puritanical" distortion of Puritanism that characterizes the abstract religious principles of Richard Digby and Parson Hooper. The Leonard Doane portion of "Alice Doane's Appeal" recounts the familiar pattern in which the projection of a sense of evil into the world is followed by the denial of that world. Walter Brome represents quite explicitly to Leonard's "diseased imagination" all the evil which Leonard feels to be potential within himself—including his own repressed desire for his sister. "My soul," Leonard confesses, "had been conscious of the germ of all the fierce and deep passions, and of all the many varieties of wickedness, which accident had brought to their full maturity in him" [285]. In killing Walter, Leonard is attempting to deny or repress his own evil imaginings. The death of Walter permits Leonard to project the question of his own guilt or innocence onto his sister and ultimately onto the whole world around him and onto his paternal and historical past.

In a sense I am only recapitulating the analysis of the psychoanalytic critics. But I find their conclusions from this analysis inadequate to the meaning of the story. Leonard's state of mind is important not simply as a "classical" example of projection or transference, but even more as an attempt on Hawthorne's part to understand psychologically how the Puritans came to be "Puritanical," how the noble intolerance of the fathers became the superstitious intolerance of the sons. Leonard's state of mind is of historical as well as of clinical importance, and the former, I would submit, is the greater of the two.

All this, after a considerable circuit, brings us back to the question of the relation of Leonard's story to the historical events of 1692. For it is his repressive "Puritanical" state of mind that links Leonard to the Salem witch trials. The victims are, insofar as their age is specified, relatively old; while many of the accusers are children. A clear emblem of the witch trials, paralleling Leonard's own guilt feelings toward his father, is the mother who, on the way to be hanged, "groaned inwardly yet with bitterest anguish, for there was her little son among the accusers" [293]. Thus the figure analogous to the villainous Cotton Mather is not Leonard's father, but Leonard himself. The state of mind that led to the hanging of innocent victims in Salem in 1692 is of a piece with the "diseased imagination" which permits Leonard to see around him only the tokens of his own repressed evil or libidinous urges. Hawthorne is fully aware of this connection. His narrative of the events in the graveyard, he points out as he turns from Leonard's story to the procession of victims and accusers in Salem, "would have brought even a church deacon to Gallows Hill, in old witch times" [292].

WHAT IS OBSCURED by confusion and sensationalism in "Alice Doane's Appeal" is revealed far more clearly in "Young Goodman Brown"—which is at once Hawthorne's most penetrating analysis of the witchcraft crisis and his most penetrating analysis of the mentality of the second and third generations of Puritans.[36]

[36] It is difficult, and rather pointless, to search for the specific historical sources of these two witchcraft stories. For one thing the actual *stories*—the adventures of Leonard Doane and Goodman Brown—are clearly not based on specific historical examples. The use of sources here, as so often in Hawthorne's historical fiction, is mainly a matter of background. This is not to say that the historical background is not important. But Hawthorne's reading in the history of witchcraft was so wide (he once planned to write a history of New England witchcraft) that it is almost always impossible to tell which details came from which source. (On this question see Dawson, *Hawthorne's Knowledge and Use of New England History*, pp. 23-24.)

The witchcraft crisis is very briefly surveyed in *Grandfather's Chair* [500-502]. Except for its relative sympathy for some of the officials involved, this account is not especially noteworthy. It casts no light on the treatment of witchcraft in "Alice Doane's Appeal" and "Young Goodman Brown." Witchcraft is also treated, rather whimsically, in "Feathertop" (1852).

For an excellent discussion of Hawthorne's accuracy in treating historical witchcraft in "Young Goodman Brown" see David Levin, *In Defense of Historical Literature*, pp. 78-87. This discussion also takes up the question, discussed in note 35 above, of the importance of "specter evidence" during the 1692 crisis.

Young Goodman Brown's journey to a Witches' Sabbath in the forest, at the time of the Salem witch trials,
is usually taken as a generalized tale of initiation, a
"timeless" allegory of the discovery of evil, of the true
nature of man. This is all very well if one feels that
Hawthorne identifies or even agrees with his protagonist. But it is not clear that Brown's one-sided vision
of the evil of the fathers and of the world in general is
any more accurate than the vision vouchsafed to Leonard Doane in the Salem graveyard. In a sense, of
course, the question of whether or not Goodman
Brown's vision is "real" is pointless: it *seems* real to
Brown and thus affects him as if it were real.[37] But
while the question of the vision's reality may be irrelevant to Brown, it is not irrelevant to the meaning of
the story. If Brown's experience in the woods is real,
then this is a tale about the depravity of mankind; and
Brown's reaction, however excessive, is morally justified. But if the experience in the woods is dreamed—
if Brown's imagination is the source of the evil from
which he retreats—then the story is hardly moral at all.
In this case Brown is not morally pure, nor is he even
innocent in any significant sense. He is simply sick.

[37] There has been considerable critical debate over the "reality"
of Goodman Brown's experience. See, for example, F. O. Matthiessen, *American Renaissance: Art and Expression in the Age of
Emerson and Whitman*, New York, 1941, p. 284; and Richard
Harter Fogle, *Hawthorne's Fiction: the Light and the Dark*, Norman, Okla., 1952, p. 18. For assertions that the whole question of
"reality" is unimportant or irrelevant see: Roy R. Male, *Hawthorne's Tragic Vision*, p. 79; Hyatt Waggoner, *Hawthorne: A
Critical Study*, pp. 60-61; and David Levin, *In Defense of Historical Literature*, p. 86.

Like Leonard Doane he is the victim of a "diseased imagination and morbid feelings."

Thus it is more than an exercise in futility to notice the evidence in the story that suggests a close relationship between the events in the woods and Brown's imagination or unconscious mind. For one thing, Brown very clearly *wakes up* at the climax of his "initiation" into evil. Hawthorne appears to equivocate at the close by asking, "Had Goodman Brown fallen asleep in the forest and only dreamed a wild dream of a witch-meeting?" [105]. To this question he answers, ambiguously, "Be it so if you will" [106]. Yet in the next sentence he refers, quite explicitly, to "the night of that fearful dream" [106]. More important than these specific references to dreaming, however, are Hawthorne's hints throughout the story that the events of Brown's experience are, as in a dream or a hallucination, produced by his own unconscious mind. For example, the devil, who significantly bears "a considerable resemblance" to Young Goodman Brown, appears only after Brown has exclaimed to himself, "What if the devil himself should be at my very elbow!" [91, 90]. When Brown resolves to walk no farther, the devil advises that they discuss the question as they proceed. But the description makes it clear that it is Brown's mind, not the devil's argument, which undermines the resolution. " 'Too far! Too far!' exclaimed the goodman, unconsciously resuming his walk" [92]. It is Brown's own naïve assertion of virtue in the world that provokes the devil into unmasking the "corruption" of Brown's townspeople and ancestors. "My father,"

78

Brown insists, virtually demanding disillusionment, "never went into the woods on such an errand, nor his father before him" [92]. We are told of the devil, a bit later, that "his arguments seemed rather to spring up in the bosom of his auditor than to be suggested by himself" [95]. When Young Goodman Brown finally has his vision of total worldly corruption in the forest, he himself projects that evil into nature: as Hawthorne expresses it, "all through the haunted forest there could be nothing more frightful than the figure of Goodman Brown" [99].

Like Richard Digby or Parson Hooper or even Leonard Doane, Young Goodman Brown is undoubtedly correct, by Hawthorne's standards, in sensing the generality of sin in the world. But he is woefully wrong, not only in his misanthropic reaction to his vision of evil, but even more in the terrible and morbid exaggeration of that vision itself. His revulsion against all human kind at the end ignores the fact that it was he himself who decided, at the outset, to enter the forest. Like Digby, Hooper, or Doane he transfers his own feelings of guilt to the outside world. He uses his vision of universal corruption to hide from himself the source of that vision, his own "sinful" urges. He becomes another of Hawthorne's fanatical and morbid escapists, beginning in self-repression and ending in self-isolation. "A stern, a sad, a darkly meditative, a distrustful, if not a desperate man," writes Hawthorne at the close, "did he become from the night of that fearful dream" [106].

Goodman Brown is a forceful example of what Hawthorne felt Puritanism became in New England. But Brown is no reflection of Hawthorne's overall judgment of New England Puritanism, as even a brief comparison with such patriarchal figures as Endicott or the Gray Champion makes clear. That the generation of Endicott would have found Brown despicable (or, if this is all a dream, that Brown fears they would) is suggested by Goody Cloyse's reference to the original Goodman Brown as "the grandfather of the silly fellow that now is" [94]. Brown represents a falling-off from the manhood of the first generation, and he knows it. And his expedition into the forest becomes a way of getting back at his ancestors for his own sense of inferiority. For if Brown's "discovery" of the evil of his father and grandfather is actually a product of Brown's own unconscious, the purpose of the forest journey (at least the *unconscious* purpose) becomes clear. Brown is unconsciously, but deliberately, undermining the hallowed image of the noble fathers that he has been taught to revere. His situation, as the son of noble ancestors, is the same as that of Edward Fitzvassal in *Nix's Mate*, and his reaction, like Fitzvassal's, involves repudiation of the fathers. Thus when Brown sees his father at the Witches' Sabbath, Hawthorne's phrasing emphasizes the subjectivity of the young man's perception. Young Goodman Brown, Hawthorne writes, "*could have well-nigh sworn* that the shape of his own dead father beckoned him to advance" [102, italics mine].

"Young Goodman Brown" does not chronicle the visitation of the sins of the fathers upon the sons. If anything it does just the opposite—as Hawthorne would feel in "The Custom-House" that his career as an author would punish his old Salem ancestors. In any case, Hawthorne is really less concerned with sin than with history. As he knew when he wrote "Main Street," the decline from the fathers to the sons was not so much a matter of the transmission of "sin" as it was an inevitable result of the principles of the founders, the conditions of life in New England, and the normal relationship of a later generation with an earlier. "Young Goodman Brown" represents, as well as any other work by Hawthorne or by his contemporaries, the proposition set forth in "Main Street" that "the sons and grandchildren of the first settlers were a race of lower and narrower souls than their progenitors had been" [460].

CHAPTER TWO

TYRANTS AND REBELS: CONVENTIONAL TREATMENTS OF INTOLERANCE

"My father never went into the woods on such an errand, nor his father before him. We have been a race of honest men and good Christians since the days of the martyrs; and shall I be the first of the name of Brown that ever took this path and kept?"—

"Such company, thou wouldst say," observed the elder person, interpreting his pause. "Well said, Goodman Brown! I have been as well acquainted with your family as with ever a one among the Puritans; and that's no trifle to say. I helped your grandfather, the constable, when he lashed the Quaker woman so smartly through the streets of Salem; and it was I that brought your father a pitch-pine knot, kindled at my own hearth, to set fire to an Indian village, in King Philip's war. They were my good friends, both. . . ."

"Young Goodman Brown"

The Narrow Puritan

HAWTHORNE'S contemporaries dealt with the apparent contradiction between the nobility and the bigotry of the Puritans by creating the opposed stereotypes of the highly principled "founding father" and the bigoted "narrow Puritan."[1] It is thus the function of the narrow Puritan, as a separate character, to explain the intolerance of the Puritans without forcing a writer altogether to abandon the myth of the heroic New England past. Such Hawthorne characters as Richard Digby and Parson Hooper, Leonard Doane and Young Goodman Brown are examples of the figure of the narrow Puritan. But with the possible exception of Richard Digby, Hawthorne's narrow Puritans are all of the second or third generation in New England—

[1] In his study of early nineteenth-century ideas about the American national character (*Cavalier and Yankee*, New York, 1961), William R. Taylor discusses the stereotype of the Yankee, as it developed in contrast to the stereotype of the Southern Cavalier. In many cases the figure of the narrow Puritan, as it appears in the books under consideration, owes a good deal to the conventional Yankee. In a few of our books—*A Peep at the Pilgrims* and *The Puritan and His Daughter* for instance—the figure of the narrow Puritan is developed in contrast with the figure of the Southerner. But for the most part, in the historical romance of early New England, the contrast is not between narrow Puritans and Southerners, but between narrow Puritans and noble Puritans. Thus, the great contrast in Cooper's *The Wept of Wish-Ton-Wish* is between Mark Heathcote and the regicide, on the one hand, and Content Heathcote and Meek Wolfe, on the other. The founding father, then, is not so much a "transcendent Yankee" (to use Professor Taylor's terms) as the complete opposite of the Yankee or narrow Puritan.

8 5

which is to say that Hawthorne is able to contain his treatment of Puritan bigotry within the larger framework of historical decline from the noble founding fathers. I will have more to say in Chapter Three about Hawthorne in this connection.

What matters here is that for most of Hawthorne's contemporaries the narrow Puritan takes on a life of his own quite apart from the figure of the noble founder—a life implying both an entirely different attitude toward Puritanism, and an entirely different reading of the direction of history. For by imputing extremes of fanaticism and hypocrisy to the first settlers, as well as to the sons and grandsons of the first settlers, the conventional figure of the narrow Puritan implies, not a myth of decline, but a myth of progress away from the errors of the fathers to the more enlightened views and practices of the nineteenth-century present. Whereas the figure of the noble founder implies an appeal to the values of the past (as is clearly the case, for example, in "The Gray Champion"), the figure of the narrow Puritan implies a rejection of the values of that past.

The portrayal of the narrow Puritan in the works of Hawthorne's contemporaries invariably raises the issue of the disjunction of appearance and reality. Sometimes the narrow Puritan is a fanatic, having exaggerated and finally distorted the fundamental reality of Puritanism. More often he is a hypocrite, using strict attention to outward appearances of piety to mask (intentionally or unintentionally) an inner state that thoroughly contradicts that character. In any case, whether fanatic, hypocrite, or both, the narrow Puritan is used again and again to exemplify the belief of nineteenth-century authors that the deplorable, repressive characteristics and actions of the first settlers of New England can be traced back to their willful or unconscious distortion of a truth now clearly seen by the enlightened nineteenth century.

If John Winthrop was the archetypal founding father, the historical archetype of the narrow Puritan was, for the nineteenth century, Cotton Mather, particularly as Mather was associated with the Salem witch trials of 1692. For our purposes a non-historical character, Mr. Conant in Lydia Maria Child's *Hobomok* (1824), will serve to illustrate the type. A harsh, ungenial man, he refuses to allow his daughter Mary to wed an Episcopalian, named Brown, and even has Brown expelled from Salem. Mary almost dies from grief, sometime later, when she hears that Brown has died in a shipwreck. Sensible of his daughter's unhappiness (and believing Brown to be dead), Conant prepares to forgive her for loving an Anglican. But finding a prayer book in her possession, he simply chastizes her once more. This final punishment drives Mary into a delirium, in the midst of which she runs off with an Indian. It is an index of Conant's fanaticism that when he hears of his daughter's madness and Indian marriage he regards them as a providential punishment, not for his cruel treatment of the girl, but for the fact that he was prepared to forgive her (and thus abet

the devilish forces of religious toleration). In Conant
fanaticism has completely triumphed over true Christianity and natural parental affection.

Hypocrisy emerges as an even more pervasive characteristic of the narrow Puritan than fanaticism. The
incongruity between pretense and practice, always potentially comic, is occasionally treated comically in
these books. Such would seem to be the entire point of
the early anonymous sketch, *Salem Witchcraft* (1820),
in which the Mathers gorge themselves on breakfast
while discoursing on the spiritual world, and in which,
for instance, a remarkably ugly woman is named
"Beautiful" Hobbes. A better example of the Puritan
hypocrite as comic figure is "the sanctimonious Benjamin Ashley" [I, 34] in Harriet Vaughan Cheney's *A
Peep at the Pilgrims* (1824). "Educated," we are told,
"in the strictest manner of his sect, he was early taught
to consider an outward conformity to its prescribed
forms, of essential importance" [I, 90]. Ashley is a
thoroughly foolish figure, his religious affectations
making him constantly the butt of ridicule, as in his
proposal to the romance's heroine. "Entreat me not to
leave thee," he pleads, "nor to return from following
after thee; for whither thou goest I will go, and where
thou diest, there will I be buried" [II, 88]. The heroine, unmoved by the feminine phrases of Ruth, turns
down this less than tempting offer. The comic incongruity of Puritan hypocrisy can also be seen in the
character (and name) of the minister, Meek Wolfe,
in Cooper's *The Wept of Wish-Ton-Wish*. The figure
of the minister in battle, sword in one hand and Bible

in the other, is clearly meant to be ridiculous. But the incongruity between Bible and sword, while it remains comic, ultimately becomes quite serious; for while Ashley fools no one, Meek Wolfe fools nearly everyone. He is a representative and leader of his society. Thus the incongruity between sword and Bible is more than a joke. It measures the extent to which Meek and his society have betrayed the true principles of their religion.

It is the threatening aspect of Puritan hypocrisy that is most often stressed in the figure of the narrow Puritan. A particularly menacing example of the type is Tobias Harpsfield, in Paulding's *The Puritan and His Daughter*. Tobias is so extreme in his hypocrisy that he, so Paulding informs the reader, "with all his circumspection could not disguise from his own heart that he was an arrant rogue." But he manages to hide this fact from the rest of the community. He is one of those, we are told, "who squared his conduct rather by the law than the gospel, and so long as he had the former on his side, dispensed with the latter. These are the most dangerous of all men to deal with" [II, 164]. Paulding makes clear just how dangerous such a man can be. Having failed to win the heart of the heroine, Tobias has her accused of witchcraft and sentenced to death for the crime. This is a long way from the ridiculous ineffectiveness of Mrs. Cheney's Benjamin Ashley. One more example of sinister hypocrisy deserves to be cited, if only for its obviousness. In *The Fair Puritan* (1844-1845) "Merciful" Whalley beats an Indian woman almost to death. Even his father, the regicide, gets the point. "Be thou Merciful, my son," he counsels, "as in name, so in deed also" [77].

In Paulding's Tobias Harpsfield is found another characteristic often (but not always) linked with Puritan hypocrisy. The real motive behind Tobias's appearance of piety is an inordinate desire for wealth. This rather naïve anticipation of Max Weber's "protestant ethic" is most thoroughly portrayed in the stepfather of the title character in Eliza Buckminster Lee's *Naomi* (1848). Mr. Aldersey comes to New England, not for liberty of conscience, but to escape prosecution for illegal financial dealings at home. He manages to double his fortune in the New World. He also manages to appear a perfect pillar of church and community. One of the secrets of his success is that on the Sabbath he privately studies market reports from abroad that no one is permitted to examine until Monday morning. "His great Bible," we are told, "lay open before him on Sunday, and upon its very leaves he wrote his commercial letters. . . . Yet his family devotions had never been apparently more fervent than upon this very evening, when his thoughts were far away, busied with commercial speculations" [31]. As such hypocrites are "Christian" only in appearance, they seize upon only the most visible manifestations of religion in their dealings with society. And most visible of all manifestations, as these romances read New England history, was the intolerant expulsion, suppression, or execution of Antinomians, Quakers, Indians, and supposed "witches."

The Sins of the Fathers:
Puritan Intolerance

It is in the suppression, exile, or slaughter of those who disagree with him that the narrow Puritan reveals the full extent of his narrowness. As the figure of the founding father embodies the patriotic myth of the heroic ancestor, so the figure of the narrow Puritan embodies the other myth of the first settlers—the myth that envisions them as having fled tyranny in England only to establish it in America. The instance of Puritan "tyranny" most obsessively treated in nineteenth-century historical romance is the witchcraft crisis of 1692. It constitutes the principal subject of more than one-third of the romances published before 1850, and minor witch trials appear in several others. But the witchcraft crisis is only one example among many of the intolerance of the Puritan founders. As we have already seen, for example, Mrs. Child treats the 1629 expulsion of Episcopalians from Salem in *Hobomok*. Motley's *Merry-Mount*, like Hawthorne's "The Maypole of Merry Mount," is concerned with the expulsion of Thomas Morton and his band of revelers from New England. The persecution of the Quakers is the main subject of Eliza Lee's *Naomi* and of John Greenleaf Whittier's *Leaves from Margaret Smith's Journal* (1849). Puritan mistreatment of Indians, finally, falls only a short way behind the witch trials in terms of the amount of treatment it receives.

It is important that Episcopalianism, Quakerism or

whatever—the particular qualities of those who are persecuted—hardly matter at all. What *does* matter is simply the fact that they are persecuted, that they oppose intolerance. For instance what matters about the Reverend William Blaxton in Motley's *Merry-Mount* is not that he is an Episcopalian, but rather that, as Motley writes, "in an age which regarded toleration as a crime, he had the courage to cultivate it as a virtue. In an age in which liberty of conscience was considered fearful licentiousness, he left his fatherland to obtain it, and was as ready to rebuke the intolerant tyranny of the nonconformist of the wilderness, as he had been to resist the bigotry and persecution of the prelacy at home" [I, 81-82]. And those accused of witchcraft, being innocent of the charge, are "witches" *only* in the sense of being victims of intolerance. Especially in this case, the particular qualities of the persecuted are irrelevant to their symbolic function as avatars of liberty in the contest with tyranny. What these persecuted figures represent, in the last analysis, is simply the "reality" to which the narrow Puritans blinded themselves.

But what, exactly, did these nineteenth-century romancers mean by "reality"? Are there any distinctive qualities, other than the fact of their being persecuted, common to the many different victims of Puritan intolerance? One gets hints of at least one such quality in the almost uniform hostility of narrow Puritans to "nature" and the "natural"—qualities often associated with the victims of intolerance. "It behooves us," announces a particularly bigoted minister in *Hobomok*, "to give little heed to natural affection, when we are engaged in the work of the Lord Jesus" [161]. Such a statement is by itself sufficient to certify a character's villainy in these books. The overwhelming importance of "nature" is clear in all of them, and it can be seen with particular clarity in the conventional portrayal of the Indian.

There is no single theme or concern behind all the different nineteenth-century treatments of seventeenth-century New England Indians. In some cases they are simply used to provide excitement—an excitement which some writers found lacking in the sermons and theological disputes that otherwise characterized the period. But the Indian was usually given the symbolic function of being yet another victim of Puritan intolerance. The most extensive example of this view of New England history is not a work of fiction, but rather Mrs. Child's *The First Settlers of New England* (1829), a didactic history intended for children. This work sets out "to prove," in the words of the author, "from the most authentic records, that the treatment [the Indians] have met with from the usurpers of their soil has been, and continues to be, in direct violation of the religious and civil institutions . . . by which we profess to be governed."[2] The high principle of the Noble Savage, in other words, exposes the hypocrisy (or false "profession") of the Puritans. Mrs. Child's purpose is, for the most part, the conventional purpose

[2] Lydia Maria Child, *The First Settlers of New-England: or, Conquest of the Pequods, Narragansetts and Pokanokets*, Boston, 1829, pp. iii-iv.

of New England historical romance with respect to the Indian. Such a Noble Savage is the Conanchet of Cooper's *Wept of Wish-Ton-Wish*. The examples are legion; one could look as well at the less developed but similarly intended figure of Uncas in the anonymous *Witch of New England* (1824).

But the treatment of the Indian also indicates the function and importance of "nature" in these books. A special feature again and again emphasized in these noble savages is their "natural" piety—a quality particularly well suited to expose by contrast the cruelty of the professedly "Christian" Puritans. This use of the savage was hardly original in the nineteenth century; one thinks, for example, of the verses in Roger Williams's *Key into the Languages of America*:

> Let none sing blessings to their souls,
>   For that they courteous are:
> The wild barbarians with no more
>   Than nature go so far.[3]

The difference in nineteenth-century literature is the worth given to "nature." Williams's poem assumes that religion, if man live by it, is definitely "more than nature." He is not attacking religious doctrine, but only men who ignore such doctrine in their daily lives even though the doctrine is available to them. For the nineteenth-century writers, however, abuse is seen as the necessary consequence of all concern with doctrine.

---

[3] Perry Miller, *Roger Williams, His Contribution to the American Tradition*, New York, 1962, p. 62. Compare Paul's remarks on those "Gentiles who have not the law," but who nonetheless "do by nature what the law requires." (Romans, 2.)

Nature, for them, is enough. The Indian, therefore, represents a religion superior to Puritanism precisely because he has turned completely from fanatical dogma to the uncluttered and uncomplicated truths of nature. For instance, Mrs. Child's Hobomok, in the book of the same name, "had never read of God, but he had heard his chariot wheels in the distant thunder, and seen his drapery in the clouds" [43]. Mrs. Child's Puritans have read of God, but that is all they have done. The opposition between the piety of the Indian and the fanaticism of the Puritan is perhaps clearest in William H. Herbert's descriptions of Merciful Whalley and his Indian slave Tituba in *The Fair Puritan*. Whalley, we are told at one point, "was, in truth, too much absorbed by his own interests . . . to give much heed to the vastness, the sublimity, the truth of nature's teachings" [82]. By contrast we are told of Tituba that she "ignorantly worshipped" God "in the roar of the cataract, in the music of the treetops, in the still majesty of solemn night, in the exulting splendor of the happy day" [91]. The point is finally expressed explicitly. "There was," Herbert writes, "more of the true, the lowly, and the grateful spirit of the Christian, in that poor, overtasked, despised, scourged heathen, than in her haughty master, who like the pharisee blessed God that he was not as other men are" [90].

The Indians are by no means the only exemplars, in this fiction, of natural piety as opposed to the narrow dogma of Puritanism. In *Naomi*, for instance, Mrs. Lee writes of the minister John Eliot, apostle to the Indians, that he possesses "a tenderness of heart opposed to the dogmas of his creed" [119]. The opposition of "heart" to "dogma" is central in this romance—especially in the opposition of the heroine, Naomi Worthington, to the harsh Puritan society of Boston. *Naomi* is concerned with the persecution of the Quakers, but the book's treatment of this dissident sect shows once again how little these writers sympathize with the particular qualities of suppressed minorities. There is a double view of Quakerism here—a view which crops up again in the Quaker Whittier's *Leaves from Margaret Smith's Journal*. Insofar as it is simply a sort of religion of the heart, the essential "truth" of Quakerism is seen as pure and beautiful. "The belief that each individual soul receives light immediately from God himself," writes Mrs. Lee, "has been the spontaneous faith of many of the purest minds throughout the world" [42]. On the other hand, Mrs. Lee is highly critical of the excesses of the Quakers, and therefore of almost all the actual seventeenth-century New England Quakers. "The Quakers," she writes, "especially the females, . . . who came to this country, were of a low order of intellect, and extremely illiterate. The principle of their religion flattered self-esteem and fostered spiritual pride, and gave to their deportment an offensive degree of arrogance and contempt for others" [336]. "Spiritual pride," in fact, seems to be a characteristic of *all* independent "females," Quaker or not. We have already been told of Anne Hutchinson, for example, that "when, from the savage solitude of her exile, she looked back upon her career, she must have feared that the slimy trail of spiritual pride had sullied the white robes of her martyrdom" [43]. Naomi, apparently, is free from this spiritual pride. Of her relationship to the Quakers we are told that "while . . . among them, she was not of them" [336]. She is punished by the intolerant Puritan society, however, for the same reasons that the "proud" Quakers are punished. We are told that Mary Dyer, the Quaker disciple of Anne Hutchinson, was hanged "to expiate the sin of thinking for herself" [177]. Naomi, we learn later, "had dared to think for herself" [391].

It is possible for Mrs. Lee to praise independence in Naomi because in her, as distinguished from Anne Hutchinson or Mary Dyer, the religion of the heart is pure. "Naomi," we are told, "although she differed altogether from the Orthodox church, held nothing in common with the Quakers of that day but the essential principle of their faith, the belief of the inward voice of truth in the soul" [336]. "She could never," Mrs. Lee notes earlier, "partake of or excuse the extravagances and follies, almost the blasphemies, of the Quakers" [104]. Naomi, then, is what Cooper would have called the *beau idéal* of historical Quakerism— she embodies the "essential principle" of the Quaker faith. What she represents is not the dogma of Quakerism as opposed to the dogma of Puritanism but rather something much more general or universal. She represents, symbolically, another variation on the idea of the "natural." And she reveals, in some detail, what the "natural" entails in these romances. For one thing, she is basically anti-intellectual. She avoids the intellectual subtleties of Puritan dogma because "nature" has "endowed her with a vigorous reason, a strong good-sense" [41]. This good sense keeps her from following the Puritans in the distortion of simple truths. And Naomi is natural in other, less obvious ways. During a Puritan service, for example, she is disturbed by the unnatural disharmony of psalm singing, an aspect of Puritanism criticized or satirized by many nineteenth-century writers. "This break in the harmony," Mrs. Lee writes, "was painful to a musical ear, but the windows of the house were open, and the waving branches of trees that were near the meeting-house supplied a continual melody to Naomi's ear, that softened the discords of inharmonious voices" [72-73]. As the "melody" of the trees is to the "discords of inharmonious voices," so is the natural, feminine good sense of Naomi to the "narrow and mistaken conceptions" [24] of the intolerant Puritans.

This contrast or conflict between nature and narrowness is essential to this romance; one scarcely exaggerates in saying it is the whole point of the book. And it is dramatically symbolized in Naomi's final trial for heresy before the Puritans, in her confidence and self-possession as she stands alone before the severity of the assembled patriarchal tribunal. Naomi is thus typical of the persecuted rebels in this fiction who represent truth as against Puritan perversion of truth. They represent reason against subtlety, good sense against obscurity. They represent, in short, the natural against the unnatural. The expulsion or execution of Quaker or Episcopalian or Indian becomes, finally, a dramatic embodiment of the denial of reason, of Christianity, of

nature on the part of the Puritan founders of New
England.

John Neal and the Salem Witch Trials

The earliest of the books under consideration to treat
witchcraft, the anonymous *Salem Witchcraft* (1820),
presents the belief in witches as a humorous example
of irrational Puritan stupidity. The Mathers, and the
other Puritans who believe in witchcraft, are presented
as ridiculous buffoons. For the most part, however, the
belief in witchcraft is treated with deadly seriousness.
But this is not to say that it is treated with much accuracy; in fact, of twelve books dealing significantly with
witchcraft (not counting Hawthorne's two witchcraft
stories), only four are set in Salem.[4] Some of the writers seem incapable of historical accuracy, as when Herbert has a character in *The Fair Puritan* speak in 1689
of those who "were" murdered at Salem [192]. What
interests these writers about the witchcraft crisis is not
the process of its development and eruption, but its
general meaning for the nineteenth-century present.

[4] Besides *Rachel Dyer*, the following books are set in Salem:
Salem Witchcraft, *The Salem Belle*, and *Zoraida: or the Witch of
Naumkeag! The Spectre of the Forest* and *Mercy Disborough* are
set in Connecticut. *The Witch of New England*, *Delusion*, and
The Puritan and His Daughter stage witch trials in unspecified
locations. In *Hope Leslie* an Indian woman is convicted of witchcraft in Springfield.

Inasmuch as most of the writers under consideration pay little
or no attention to the events in Salem, the question of historical
sources is essentially irrelevant. It is interesting to note, however,
that Robert Calef's 1700 attack on the Mathers and their part in
the crisis, *More Wonders of the Invisible World*, was reprinted in
1823.

And by and large the witch trials are seen as yet another instance—the most terrifying instance of all—of the Puritan persecution of innocent victims.

The main exception to this generalization is, of course, Hawthorne. He is hardly concerned with the innocence of the victims. In *The Scarlet Letter*, for instance, Mistress Hibbins believes herself to be a witch and is quite sure she meets the devil in the forest. And such meetings with the devil are the principal subject of both "Alice Doane's Appeal" and "Young Goodman Brown," Hawthorne's main fictional portrayals of witches. To be sure, Hawthorne does not himself assume the "reality" of witchcraft; at least I have argued that the Witches' Sabbaths are figments of the imaginations of Leonard and Goodman Brown. But the fact remains that Hawthorne is much more interested in the situation of those who think themselves or others to be witches than in the situation of the innocent accused. And thus Hawthorne's treatment of witchcraft is almost unique; it sets him quite apart from his contemporaries, for whom the witch trials, as material for fiction, are not essentially different from the kinds of intolerance discussed so far. There is, however, a difference in intensity of treatment. There is a kind of fury in the presentation of the witch trials not usually found in the treatment of other forms of persecution. Both the fury and the intensity are probably clearest in John Neal's romance of the Salem witch trials, *Rachel Dyer: A North American Story* (1828).

Neal's Rachel Dyer and her sister Elizabeth are, like Naomi Worthington or Mary Conant, innocent victims of Puritan bigotry. Their symbolic importance is emphasized by the fact that Neal has made them grandchildren of Mary Dyer, one of the Quakers hanged on Boston Common. But the real focus of *Rachel Dyer*, in spite of its title, is on the hero, George Burroughs, a minister who returns from Maine to Salem to defy the court, and whose defiance leads to his own execution as a "witch." There is a good deal of Gothic sensationalism in *Rachel Dyer*, especially during Burroughs's trial; but beneath its often hysterical surface the book is obviously meant as an indictment of the injustice of the witch trials of 1692. During the trial of Martha Cory, whom he has returned to Salem to defend, Burroughs describes a Utopia that exposes the inequities of the Puritans:

a nation . . . where all men were supposed by the law to be innocent, until they were *proved* to be guilty, . . . where the verdict of at least twelve, and in some cases of twenty-four men—their unanimous verdict too, was required for the condemnation of such accused; where if a man where [*sic*, read "were"] charged with a crime, he was not even permitted to accuse himself . . . , till he had been put upon his guard by the judges. . . . [104]

The main features of this Utopia, one sees, are the constitutional liberties of nineteenth-century America, and the implication is that nineteenth-century America has progressed from the days in which a George Burroughs could be hanged for opposing the illegal mandates of an arbitrary court. The implication that Burroughs is somehow representative of progress toward the present is strengthened by a statement about Burroughs that

101

Neal attributes to "an old writer of America": "He appeared on earth . . . about a hundred years too soon. What he was put to death for in 1692, he may be renowned for (if it please the Lord) in 1792" [149]. Neal continues in his own voice, to drive the point home: "He should have made war—he might have been a leader of armies—a legislator—a statesman—a deliverer. Had he appeared in the great struggle for North-American liberty, fourscore years later, he probably would have been all this" [150]. The judges of 1692, however, ignore this representative of the future. To all his arguments they answer with five words: "*The—wisdom—of—our—ancestors*" [122]. Burroughs defying the court seems clearly intended as an emblem of the future (or nineteenth-century present) defying the past.

And yet a reading of *Rachel Dyer* as a book affirming progress encounters immediate difficulties. If it is true that Burroughs represents an enlightened present as opposed to a superstitious past, it is equally true that he does not triumph over that past and is, in fact, destroyed by it. We find in the destruction of Burroughs not the affirmation of progress but those qualities that Harold Martin has found to be typical of Neal's work in general: "the arrogance, the sentimentality, the near-paranoia, . . . the rage against order and the frenzy in chaos—all the poses of the romantic."[5] The most notable of these qualities in *Rachel Dyer* is surely the paranoia; the more hysterically he protests—and this is

---

[5] Harold C. Martin, "The Colloquial Tradition in the Novel: John Neal," *New England Quarterly*, XXXII (1959), 458.

among the most hysterical of books—the less effective
Burroughs becomes in evading alienation and destruction. At the end of the book the entire society of Salem
is marshaled against him. John D. Seelye has noted that
Neal probably meant Burroughs as "something of a
self-portrait," and has suggested further that Burroughs's paraonia reflects Neal's sense of his own isolation as a man of imagination in provincial Portland—
as, therefore, "a victim of small-town persecution."[6]
This may be true, but it seems to me that Burroughs's
paranoia represents as well problems that may have lain
even deeper in Neal's mind. I would suggest that the
destruction of Burroughs, like the destruction of Edward Fitzvassal in *Nix's Mate*, reveals something of the
frustration and confusion of the generation of American novelists writing in the demeaning shadow of the
heroic revolutionary fathers. When Neal notes that
Burroughs had all the qualities of a revolutionary hero,
he is not simply saying that Burroughs was born *before*
his time. More generally he is describing Burroughs as
a man of greatness who lived at the *wrong* time—a
Washington in an age of inferior possibilities. It is with
this more general notion of Burroughs's situation, I
would suggest, that Neal identified. It is this post-
revolutionary frustration, I think, much more than the
legal irregularity of the 1692 trials, that lies behind the
hysteria of so much of *Rachel Dyer*. In this light the
judges' withering reply to Burroughs's protests—"*The
—wisdom—of—our—ancestors*"—acquires a new sig-

[6] John D. Seelye, Introduction to *Rachel Dyer . . . by John Neal*,
Gainesville, Fla., 1964, pp. x, viii.

nificance. Burroughs is defeated not so much by superstition as by filiopietism.

It is a curious instance of Neal's confusion that he himself, in the July Fourth oration delivered ten years after *Rachel Dyer*, gave voice to exactly the sort of filiopietism that destroys Burroughs. "Just in proportion as we have departed from the usages of our fathers—" he declared in 1838, "exactly in that proportion have we been afflicted as a people."[7] Like Rufus Dawes, Neal could both accept and rebel against the myth of decline from the fathers. And as with *Nix's Mate*, so with *Rachel Dyer* one cannot be sure how fully the author intended his tragic hero as a projection of his own frustration. The author-hero parallel is much clearer in *Nix's Mate* than in *Rachel Dyer*. But even in *Rachel Dyer* the parallel is there, suggesting not only Neal's ambivalence toward the myth of the founding fathers but also suggesting—what is more important for our purposes—the peculiar problems apparently connected with the use of a male rebel as a hero for New England historical romance. One might note, in closing, that of all the books to treat witchcraft *Rachel Dyer* is quite alone in presenting the accusation and trial of a man for the crime. It is also the only "tragedy": of all the heroines accused and convicted of witchcraft, not one is finally executed.

[7] John Neal, *Oration, July 4, 1838*, Portland, Me., 1838, p. 24.

CHAPTER THREE

A HOME IN THE WILDERNESS: HAWTHORNE'S HISTORICAL THEMES

"Fellow-soldiers,—fellow-exiles," began Endicott, . . . "wherefore did ye leave your native country? Wherefore, I say, have we left the green and fertile fields, the cottages, or, perchance, the old gray halls, where we were born and bred, the churchyards where our forefathers lie buried? Wherefore have we come hither to set up our own tombstones in a wilderness?"

"Endicott and the Red Cross"

So said Hester Prynne, and glanced her sad eyes downward at the scarlet letter. And, after many, many years, a new grave was delved, near an old and sunken one. . . . Yet one tombstone served for both.

The Scarlet Letter

"Take heart, child, and tell me what is your name and where is your home?"

"Friend," replied the little boy, in a sweet though faltering voice, "they call me Ilbrahim, and my home is here."

"The Gentle Boy"

Hawthorne's Attitude Toward Puritanism

IT IS NOT SURPRISING that the crucial issue in understanding the Puritans was for Hawthorne, as for his contemporaries, the intolerance of the heroic Puritan founding fathers. That this issue had particular relevance for Hawthorne, the descendant of these founders, is clear throughout his historical fiction, especially in the famous passage in "The Custom-House" describing the first Salem Hathorne[1] and his son:

He was . . . a bitter persecutor; as witness the Quakers, who have remembered him in their histories, and relate an incident of his hard severity towards a woman of their sect. . . . His son, too, inherited the persecuting spirit, and made himself so conspicuous in the martyrdom of the witches, that their blood may fairly be said to have left a stain upon him. [9]

Hawthorne did not, however, simply criticize his founding-father ancestors. In this same passage he notes of the first Hawthorne that in spite of his severity his "better deeds . . . were many." "He had all the Puritanic traits," Hawthorne concludes, "both good and evil" [9]. Hawthorne had, in short, a balanced view of his forebears. He was able to see both the "good" and

---

[1] Hawthorne himself added the "w" to the family name when he began to publish—perhaps (as has been suggested) to distinguish himself from his ancestors, but more probably, it seems to me, to remove the ambiguity of pronunciation in the original spelling ("Hay"thorne vs. "Haw"thorne)—an ambiguity which would severely inconvenience an obscure author hoping to make his name known.

the "evil" in the founders of New England. He was able to admire their nobility even while censuring their intolerant severity.

This attitude hardly makes Hawthorne unique among early nineteenth-century American writers. This is, in fact, the same double view of the founders that produced the central tension in the historical romance of New England—and thus also produced the opposed stereotypes of founding father and narrow Puritan. One need not look very far to find these opposed stereotypes in Hawthorne's fiction as well. The movement from noble father to superstitious son is central to Hawthorne's portrayal of seventeenth-century New England history. Less frequently one finds Hawthorne placing the conventional opposition between noble founder and narrow Puritan within the first generation itself—as in the following tableau from "Mrs. Hutchinson":

Here are collected all those blessed fathers of the land, who rank in our veneration next to the evangelists of Holy Writ; and here, also, are many, unpurified from the fiercest errors of the age, and ready to propagate the religion of peace by violence. In the highest place sits Winthrop,— a man by whom the innocent and guilty might alike desire to be judged; the first confiding in his integrity and wisdom, the latter hoping in his mildness. Next is Endicott, who would stand with his drawn sword at the gate of heaven, and resist to the death all pilgrims thither, except they travelled his own path. [223]

This opposition of Winthrop and Endicott is every bit as conventional as the description of Winthrop and

Dudley in Motley's *Merry-Mount*, quoted at the beginning of Chapter One.

But such conventional oppositions between members of the first generation of Puritans are rare in Hawthorne, and the reasons for their rarity are important. Hawthorne's contemporaries, by and large, wished to glorify the New England past, and thus their attitude toward the founders, their ability to praise or need to blame them, had a direct effect on their fiction. Hawthorne appears to have been less interested in judging the past than in understanding it on its own terms. If the past contained contradictions, Hawthorne was primarily interested not in resolving those contradictions, but in comprehending their historical relationship. In terms of the whole history of the seventeenth century in New England this "historical relationship" between nobility and intolerance involved a process of decline from fathers to sons. But in facing those fathers themselves—the members of the first generation—Hawthorne realized that the intolerance could not be isolated, as it *was* conventionally isolated in the figure of the narrow Puritan. To understand the nobility of the fathers, for Hawthorne, required an understanding of their bigotry as well—and an understanding of how the nobility and bigotry were intertwined.

This unified view of the founders can be seen in "Endicott and the Red Cross." Endicott's "liberty" involves both courageous independence and self-righteous intolerance. In the tableau of magistrates in "Mrs. Hutchinson" Hawthorne allows himself the easy stereotype of Endicott as narrow Puritan, as opposed to the

noble Winthrop. But in the fuller treatment of Endicott in "Endicott and the Red Cross" Hawthorne is
working at a deeper level. He is working from the
realization—missed or avoided by most of his contemporaries—that for a man like Endicott the qualities of
courage and bigotry were not contradictory, and thus
to understand such a man (and what he represents for
America) one must *accept* the combination of these
qualities. One must then work from such an acceptance
to an exploration of how the qualities came to be combined, and what their combination has meant for those
who have succeeded Endicott—including Nathaniel
Hawthorne. Which is to say that Hawthorne's treatment of Puritan intolerance is less directly ethical than
that of his contemporaries, and more historical. What
I mean here by "historical" may be clarified by discuss-
ing the historical themes of "The Gentle Boy." This
tale is particularly appropriate here, since it is frequently used to demonstrate Hawthorne's balanced attitude
toward Puritanism.[2]

[2] According to Edward Dawson, "The Gentle Boy" relies most
heavily on William Sewel's *History of the Quakers*—Hawthorne's
Catharine being a sort of collation of four women described by
Sewel: Elizabeth Hooten, Mary Dyer, Mary Fisher, and Catherine
Evans. (*Hawthorne's Knowledge and Use of New England History*, Nashville, Tenn., 1939, pp. 20-21.) But once again Hawthorne's accuracy is primarily a matter of background. The story
of Tobias and Ilbrahim, although a profound expression of Hawthorne's ideas about seventeenth-century history, does not appear
to be based on any historical sources. "The Gentle Boy" was first
published in the *Token* in 1832, and collected in *Twice-Told Tales*
in 1837.

For discussion of Hawthorne's balanced attitude toward Puritanism, see especially Barriss Mills, "Hawthorne and Puritanism,"

The balance in this story is obvious. On the one hand it is quite critical of Puritan intolerance. The protagonist, Tobias Pearson, is ostracized from the Puritan community for adopting the child of an executed Quaker, to take the place of his own children who perished after coming to the New World. Further, in spite of Pearson's efforts the little Quaker, Ilbrahim, dies as a result of the cruelty of the Puritan children. Hawthorne does not excuse this cruelty. But neither, on the other hand, does he sentimentalize or even admire the persecuted Quakers. Ilbrahim's mother, Catharine, abandons her son in order to spread the Quaker version of "truth" through the wilderness. Hawthorne makes it clear that she shares equally with the Puritans the responsibility for Ilbrahim's death. And Hawthorne's attitude toward Catharine is matched by a general skepticism about the Quakers. "The command of the spirit," he writes, "inaudible except to the soul, and not to be controverted on grounds of human wisdom, was made a plea for most indecorous exhibitions, which, abstractedly considered, well deserved the moderate chastisement of the rod" [86]. The crime of the Puritans lay not in punishing the innocent, but in excessively punishing the guilty.[3]

New England Quarterly, XXI (1948), 78-102; and J. Golden Taylor, *Hawthorne's Ambivalence Toward Puritanism*, Logan, Utah (Utah State University Press, Monograph Series, XII, 1), 1965.

[3] In his perceptive discussion of the 1837 revision of "The Gentle Boy" Seymour L. Gross concludes that one effect of the revisions is that of "solidifying . . . a remarkably perilous balance between Puritan and Quaker." "Hawthorne," he continues, "manip-

Hawthorne did not, of course, write "The Gentle Boy" simply to express his opinions of Puritans or Quakers. Rather he used his knowledge of Puritans and Quakers to provide the context for the individual tragedies of Tobias and Ilbrahim. But in Hawthorne's historical fiction the creation of tragedy, even individual tragedy, is very much a matter of history. "The Gentle Boy" can be read as a "timeless" tale of human suffering, but it is far more profoundly a story set at a particular time, at a particular moment in American history. It begins with an account of different motives which led different groups to migrate to the New World and then proceeds to set forth the ways in which these groups and their original motives are altered by the conditions of their survival (or failure to survive) in the New World environment. This is the great theme of Hawthorne's historical fiction. When he collected his essays on English life in 1863, Hawthorne entitled the collection *Our Old Home*. "The Gentle Boy," like so much of Hawthorne's historical fiction, deals with the interplay of Old World values and New World conditions—with the establishment of a "home" in the wilderness, our *new* home.[4]

---

ulated his material, especially through his revisions, so as to point up the mutuality of guilt." ("Hawthorne's Revision of 'The Gentle Boy,'" *American Literature*, xxvi [1954], 196, 208.)

[4] Compare Roy R. Male's statement about "The Gentle Boy" that its "subject is the agonizing difficulty of finding an integrated, fruitful religious experience in America—the difficulty, that is to say, of finding a home." (*Hawthorne's Tragic Vision*, New York, 1957, p. 45.) I am very much indebted to this excellent study.

Thus the land through which Tobias Pearson walks at the beginning of the story is still, in 1659, largely wilderness. "The tracts of original forest," we are told, "still bore no small proportion to the cultivated ground" [87]. Tobias's journey in this wilderness becomes a symbolic quest. "A gloomy extent of nearly four miles lay between [the traveler] and his home" [87], writes Hawthorne in 1837, substituting the word "home" for the 1832 reading, "house."[5] When Tobias finds Ilbrahim on a fresh grave he asks the child, "Where is your home?" And the child replies, "My home is here" [89]. Tobias has a different sort of future in mind for his adopted son. "Look up, child," he announces as they approach the Pearson house, "there is our home." "At the word 'home,'" Hawthorne writes, "a thrill passed through the child's frame" [92]. "The Gentle Boy" chronicles the steady deterioration of Tobias's ability to fulfill his promise to Ilbrahim. This process is made tangible in the physical deterioration of Pearson's house—the "home" to which Ilbrahim is welcomed at the outset. At first it is notable for its warmth and prosperity, but both soon disappear. "The apartment," we are told of Pearson's front room by the time of Ilbrahim's death, "was saddened in its aspect by the absence of much of the homely wealth which had once adorned it" [115]. At the close of the tale we learn that years later Ilbrahim's mother Catharine, chastened by her loss, returned "to Pearson's dwelling and made that her home" [125]. But there has been a profound trans-

[5] Gross, "Hawthorne's Revision of 'The Gentle Boy,'" p. 199n.

formation, and this later "home" is a different, sadder place from the "home" that sent a thrill through the frame of Ilbrahim.

That this transformation is specifically historical as well as generally tragic is first evident in the story's concern with the effect of the migration on the original purposes of the Puritans and Quakers. In both cases the initial purpose has been severely distorted by the conditions of the New World. The Quakers, who preach love and peace, receive and provoke violence; and Catharine, in the name of love, abandons her child. The Puritans, as in so much of the conventional romance of New England, are portrayed as having fled tyranny in the Old World only to establish it themselves in the New. But in terms of the story the most important impact of the wilderness is on the plans of Tobias Pearson. One of Pearson's reasons for migrating is his belief that Cromwell betrayed the cause in England through personal ambition. A more important reason has to do with Pearson's expectations about life in the New World. "New England," we are told, "offered advantages to men of unprosperous fortunes, as well as to dissatisfied religionists, and Pearson had hitherto found it difficult to provide for a wife and increasing family" [94]. Thus the decline of Pearson's fortunes, resulting from his ostracism, is emblematic of the collapse of the way of life he has projected for himself and his family in New England. Even before the story begins some hostile quality in the New World has killed all of Pearson's children.

Children are of obvious importance in this tale—not

only Ilbrahim and the departed Pearson children, but also the intolerant Puritan children whose cruelty is the direct cause of Ilbrahim's death. Hawthorne uses these children not only as actors in the story but as symbols, in the fictional present, of the historical future.[6] Or, more precisely, one might say that these children represent conflicting elements struggling in the Darwinian sense to see which will survive to *become* the future. The little Puritans represent the element that will survive. They will go on to outdo even their fathers in suspicion and intolerance. As opposed to these little Puritans, Ilbrahim and the departed Pearson children represent a future projected from the Old World but for some reason impossible in the New. These children represent a certain fullness or beauty of life for which Hawthorne twice in this tale chooses the image of the dying rose. As the beaten Ilbrahim lies dying in bed we are told that he pined and drooped "like a cankered rosebud" [115]. Of the Pearson children Hawthorne writes that "they had left their native country blooming like roses, and like roses they had perished in a foreign soil" [94]. The image of the transplanted rosebush expresses the whole movement of the story, and the tragedy, not only of Pearson and Ilbrahim, but of the entire Puritan migration. The roses, and the dying children, are associated with Old World possibilities

---

[6] Compare Hawthorne's description of "Grandfather" talking to his young listeners in *Grandfather's Chair*: "When he talked to them, it was the past speaking to the present, or rather to the future,—for the children were of a generation which had not become actual" [478].

stunted by the conditions of the New World.[7] After
Tobias and his wife adopt Ilbrahim we are told that
"their affection for him became like the memory of
their native land, or their mild sorrow for the dead"
[107].

"The Gentle Boy" is a very simple story. Like James,
if with less firsthand experience, Hawthorne early came
to associate "life" with Europe, with the Old World.
In the New World, as Hawthorne read American history, this "life" somehow withered away; it perished in
the soil of the wilderness. This process of withering was
important to Hawthorne because, as he saw it, his own
America was its result. The conditions of nineteenth-
century America were determined, in a large part,
by the sort of home the Puritans made in the wilderness. Thus nineteenth-century America, in Hawthorne's
analysis, was somehow insubstantial as compared with
England. American life was thinner, less robust than
English life. This difference in life styles was the result
of an historical process, and this process forms, again
and again, the main subject of Hawthorne's historical
fiction. Thus "The Gentle Boy" charts the withering
of Tobias Pearson's hope for a full life in America—or,

[7] One might compare to this the description of Endicott's beautiful wife in "Main Street" as "a rose of beauty from an English
garden, now to be transplanted to a fresher soil" [447]. The
"showman" in "Main Street" waxes enthusiastic over her contribution to the beauty of the American race, but a listener interrupts
to point out "that Anna Gower, the first wife of Governor Endicott,
and who came with him from England, left no posterity" [448].
In *Grandfather's Chair* "Grandfather" describes Lady Arbella
Johnson, who died shortly after arriving in New England, as "fading away, like a pale English flower, in the shadow of the forest!"
[440].

more precisely, it charts the failure of Pearson's last attempt to recapture that hope. Pearson's dream of a prosperous home in the wilderness becomes identified with the child to whom he promises such a home. Thus when Ilbrahim dies the point is, not that either the Puritans or the Quakers should assume the blame, but rather that "home" in America could not, after the migration, mean precisely what it had meant in England. The home to which Catharine returns at the end (like the home to which Hester Prynne returns at the end of *The Scarlet Letter*) is a very different place from the sort of home Tobias promises to Ilbrahim. It is one of the overriding concerns of Hawthorne's historical fiction of New England to try to set forth and comprehend this difference. The transformation of the English character in the American wilderness becomes, one may say, Hawthorne's principal historical theme.

Thus the characteristic tension in Hawthorne's fiction of New England is not between nobility and intolerance, but rather between Old World values and New World conditions. For instance, in the historical sketch "Main Street," as in "The Gentle Boy," the separation of the Puritans from England results, in the New World, in a loss of richness and beauty. The Puritan forefathers, we are told, "wove their web of life with hardly a single thread of rose-color or gold" [471]. The separation is irrevocable, but it is still, in the first generation, somewhat incomplete. Some qualities of Old World life still survive in the New World. In this respect the house of Roger Conant, the first settler of Salem, is significant: "There stands his habitation," the showman-narrator declares, "showing in its rough architecture some features of the Indian wigwam, and some of the log-cabin, and somewhat, too, of the straw-thatched cottage in Old England, where this good yeoman had his birth and breeding" [443]. At the beginning of the seventeenth century, as Hawthorne presents New England history, qualities of both old home and New World were still mingled in the wilderness. It was only with the passage of time that the qualities of the old home were completely expelled.

This process of expulsion forms the main subject of "Endicott and the Red Cross." The essence of Endicott's "liberty" is a rejection of all things English—not only English domination but also English values, not only "tyranny" but also warmth and gaiety. Endicott's "liberty" requires not only the cutting of the red cross from the banner of England, but also the suppression of the reveler who had "boisterously quaffed a health to the king" [468] and the woman with the scarlet A on her gown. Even Endicott is aware of what has been lost through the separation from England. "Wherefore," he asks at the beginning of his impassioned oration, "did ye leave your native country? Wherefore, I say, have we left the green and fertile fields, the cottages, or, perchance, the old grays halls, where we were born and bred, the churchyards where our forefathers lie buried? Wherefore have we come hither to set up our own tombstones in a wilderness?" [491]. Endicott ultimately answers his question in action, and his action determines that the qualities left behind in England shall from now on be permanently estranged from American life.

The tension or contest between Old and New World values in the wilderness is of crucial importance in another Hawthorne story involving Endicott, "The Maypole of Merry Mount." "The Maypole of Merry Mount" is based on the same historical events that lie behind John Lothrop Motley's *Merry-Mount*—the conflict between the stern Puritans of New England and the revelers who lived under Thomas Morton at Merry Mount until they were expelled by their foes.[8] Motley adds to this material all the trappings of romance. Hawthorne's principal addition is a young couple, Edith and Edgar, who are converted from the ways of Merry Mount to the ways of Plymouth. "The Maypole of Merry Mount," with its stylized opposition of light and darkness, is generally (and quite correctly) read as a psychological fable—as an allegory of the opposition of heart and head, of unbridled sensuality and

[8] Motley's romance appeared thirteen years after "The Maypole of Merry Mount." But Motley insisted in his preface that he had not read Hawthorne's tale. Much of the description of the revels at Merry Mount is based on Strutt's *Sports and Pastimes* (1801). Hawthorne could have found what little historical information the tale contains (the existence of Morton's band, Endicott's cutting down the Maypole) in Bradford's *Plymouth Plantation*. (See Dawson, *Hawthorne's Knowledge and Use of New England History*, pp. 14-16.) Edith and Edgar, needless to say, are figments of Hawthorne's imagination. Hawthorne has somewhat telescoped the historical record here. Endicott broke up Morton's revelers, and then *later* returned to chop down the Maypole. For obvious reasons, both dramatic and symbolic, Hawthorne has these two separate events occur simultaneously.

119

iron repression. Neither psychological extreme, in the scheme of the story, is satisfactory on its own. The Puritans—creatures of darkness and "most dismal wretches" [77]—are so hostile to impulse that they have completely cut themselves off from life. At the other extreme the hedonism of the revelers, as it ignores mutability and inevitable sorrow, is no more satisfactory. Edgar and Edith, the Lord and Lady of the May, are apparently intended to represent a kind of ideal mean between the extremes of repression and sensuality. Thus even before the appearance of the Puritans they realize the insufficiency of the Merry Mounters' hedonism. They are already prepared to follow Endicott to Plymouth. There, presumably, their love, not to mention their previous experience, will keep them from the extremes of Puritan repression. True happiness or psychological adjustment, the story seems to say, consists in balancing the claims of the heart and head. Neither faculty should be denied.

But the fable of "The Maypole of Merry Mount" is historical as well as psychological. Light and darkness are not simply allegorical representations of psychological faculties; they are also forces at work in history, in the history of the beginnings of America. "Jollity and gloom," Hawthorne writes in the opening paragraph, "were contending for an empire" [70]. The importance of the historical consequences of this contention is suggested at greater length during a later discussion of the feud between revelers and Puritans:

The future complexion of New England was involved in this important quarrel. Should the grizzly saints establish their jurisdiction over the gay sinners, then would their spirits darken all the clime, and make it a land of clouded visages, of hard toil, of sermon and psalm forever. But should the banner staff of Merry Mount be fortunate, sunshine would break upon the hills, and flowers would beautify the forest, and late posterity do homage to the Maypole. [78-79]

This passage, particularly in its use of light and dark imagery, is curiously conventional. In many of the works of Hawthorne's contemporaries light and dark are used to symbolize historical progress from the intolerance of the Puritans to the clear reason of the nineteenth-century present. Mrs. Lee, who is addicted to dawn imagery for precisely this reason, writes of the hero at the end of *Naomi* that he "waited patiently in the darkness, tarrying for the dawn. Truth and justice came at length. He waited not in vain" [448]. Similarly, she writes of her hero at the end of *Delusion* that he at last "stood in the clear sunshine of reason" [159].

In "The Maypole of Merry Mount," too, a young couple associated with light and gaiety is opposed by a severe tyrant associated with intolerance and darkness. But here the similarity between Hawthorne's story and the conventional works of his contemporaries ends. For Edith and Edgar capitulate completely to Endicott's authority, and what is more we are made to feel that they are right to do so. Whereas romance after romance celebrates the "dawn" of reason, "The Maypole of Merry Mount" takes place at sunset. "With the setting sun," we are told, "the last day of mirth had passed from Merry Mount" [79]. Thus "The Maypole

of Merry Mount" presents the conventional contest between intolerance and reason, darkness and light, but
it gives that contest an unconventional outcome. "The
moral gloom of the world," Hawthorne writes at the
close, "overpowers all systematic gaiety" [84]. This is
a general statement about the nature of things. But it
is also a statement about what happened at a particular time in history when "jollity and gloom were contending for an empire." Gloom, quite simply, won.

It is important to note, finally, how consistently in
this story the forces of jollity and gloom are associated,
respectively, with the opposed life styles of Old World
and New World. In a sense "The Maypole of Merry
Mount" is simply a more abstract rendering of the central event of "Endicott and the Red Cross"—the repudiation of England to establish an American character.
A significant difference between the two stories is that
in "The Maypole of Merry Mount" the severity of the
Puritans is not tempered with patriotic associations.
Divested of nationalistic connotations, the conflicting
life styles of the rival groups must struggle (again in
the Darwinian sense) on their own merits. The association of the revelers with England is unmistakable.
"All the hereditary pastimes of Old England," we are
told, and the metaphor is significant, "were transplanted hither" [76]. The revelers observe all the traditional holidays of their old home. Of the Puritans we
are told, by contrast, that "when they met in conclave,
it was never to keep up the old English mirth, but to
hear sermons three hours long, or to proclaim bounties
on the heads of wolves and the scalps of Indians. Their

festivals were fast days, and their chief pastime the singing of psalms" [77]. In "Endicott and the Red Cross" Endicott protested the rumored intention of Charles I and Archbishop Laud "to establish the idolatrous forms of English Episcopacy" in New England [492]. The revels at Merry Mount are presided over by "an English priest, canonically dressed, yet decked with flowers."[9] In this priest, who "seemed the wildest monster there, and the very Comus of the crew" [73], the sensualism of the revelers is most clearly associated with the effort to establish the forms and styles of English, as opposed to Puritan, life in the New World.

"The Maypole of Merry Mount" presents a struggle, not between Old England and New, but finally between two possible New World futures—one an effort to hold to old ways, and the other an effort to strike out in new, independent directions. Thus the revelers represent,

[9] Endicott identifies this priest as "Blackstone," an Anglican cleric who lived at the future site of Boston during the 1620's (and who is used sympathetically by Motley as a spokesman for liberty of conscience in *Merry-Mount*). The identification of the retiring recluse with this "Comus" is so preposterous that Hawthorne himself adds a note apologizing for Endicott's "mistake." Terence Martin notes that in the first (1836) version of the story the priest was identified as "Claxton," meaning Laurence Claxton (or Clarkson) who, Martin writes, "though he was never in the colonies, was known as a ranter and an Anabaptist who tolerated Maypoles." (*Nathaniel Hawthorne*, New York, 1965, p. 87.) Even in this earlier version Hawthorne questioned Endicott's identification in a note. Martin sees the change to Blackstone as an effort further to undermine Endicott's reliability. My own guess, however, would be that Hawthorne made the change in order to intensify the identification of the sensual life of the revelers with the English religious forms rejected by the Puritans—rather than with the vagaries of other divergent sects.

not the true gaiety of the Old World, but a hopeless attempt to deny that this gaiety has been irrevocably lost. They are not Europeans in America so much as Americans trying in vain to be Europeans. "The men of whom we speak," writes Hawthorne, "after losing the heart's fresh gayety, imagined a wild philosophy of pleasure" [75]. As in "The Gentle Boy" so here, too, the effort to revive the Old World in the New is associated with flowers, and especially with roses. The priest is "decked with flowers" [73], and the Maypole is hung with "an abundant wreath of roses" [71]. This wreath is to be thrown over the heads of Edith and Edgar, solemnizing not only their marriage but the revelers' plans for the New World as well. The Puritans enter before this moment in the ceremony, however, and Endicott hews down the Maypole, the "flower-decked abomination" [80]. Yet when he turns to Edith and Edgar, we are told, "the iron man was softened" [83]. He demonstrates his compassion in a curious symbolic gesture. "And Endicott," Hawthorne writes, "the severest Puritan of all who laid the rock foundation of New England, lifted the wreath of roses from the ruin of the Maypole, and threw it, with his own gauntleted hand, over the heads of the Lord and Lady of the May" [84]. At the last minute Endicott himself completes the ceremony begun by the "English priest"—before leading the couple off to a new life at Plymouth. The story ends, or seems intended to end, in balance and hope—a hope underlined by the insistent echoes, as Edith and Edgar are led from Merry Mount, of the ending of *Paradise Lost.*

In spite of the apparent neatness of this ending, it presents problems to the reader who has found the vision of conflict between light and dark more convincing than the final attempt at resolution. In terms of the overall form of the tale the apparent resolution of conflict embodied in Edith and Edgar functions more as a smoke screen than as a true conclusion. The concentration on this ideal couple at the end, suggesting a kind of balance between the extremes of sensuality and repression, jollity and gloom, obscures the fact that no such balance has been achieved in the story. The party of gloom has triumphed completely. If there is anything like balance in this ending, it is in the final kindness of Endicott. Here we have a faint vision of a more hopeful reading of the triumph of the Puritans, a vision in which the Puritans' stern but necessary rejection of England chastens the sensuality of the Old World without absolutely eradicating it. Perhaps the American future might be balanced in this sense. If so, the New World would represent the ideal compromise—a kind of earthly paradise. But this ideal is at best tenuous. The Miltonic echoes at the end of the story suggest rather strongly that if there is a paradise Edith and Edgar are *leaving* it. Endicott's compromise cannot be permanent because it is not, symbolically, in character—an important point in a story where characterization is largely a matter of symbolism. Endicott is a man of iron, not of flowers. His sympathetic gesture obscures the fact that he has triumphed. While Hawthorne does not deplore this triumph, and in fact sees it as both an historical and a psychological necessity, he nonetheless regrets its consequences. He regrets what has been lost. In fact it is regret, rather than a change of heart, that moves Endicott at the close. "He almost sighed," we are told, "for the inevitable blight of early hopes" [83]. The blight, it is clear, is no less inevitable for the sigh. Whether we regret it or not, the loss remains, and it is in this sense that "The Maypole of Merry Mount" is fundamentally an "historical" story. Edith and Edgar will lead more responsible, perhaps more meaningful lives in Plymouth. But they will not find roses among the Puritans.

A New World: The Scarlet Letter

The action of the *The Scarlet Letter* takes place entirely in a small New World settlement at the edge of a wilderness, far from the court and aristocracy of Old England. Thus the book's closing emphasis on heraldry, the symbolism of aristocracy, seems a bit curious. It may be appropriate that Pearl, who has apparently married into some noble continental family, should send her mother "letters . . . with armorial seals upon them, though of bearings unknown to English heraldry" [262]. But the closing paragraph, describing Hester's tomb in the Boston graveyard, applies heraldry to the New World as well:

All around, there were monuments carved with armorial bearings; and on this simple slab of slate—as the curious investigator may still discern, and perplex himself with the purport—there appeared the semblance of an engraved escutcheon. It bore a device, a herald's wording of which might serve for a motto and brief description of our now

concluded legend; so sombre is it, and relieved only by one
ever-glowing point of light gloomier than the shadow: —

"ON A FIELD, SABLE, THE LETTER A, GULES."

[264]

The peculiar relevance of this ending to the romance
as a whole can be seen if one turns back, briefly, to the
opening scene—Hester's exposure on the scaffold. In
the midst of her humiliation Hester's mind wanders to
recollections of her old home in England. She recalls
her infancy, her mother, her "father's face, with its bald
brow, and reverend white beard, that flowed over the
old-fashioned Elizabethan ruff." Of particular interest
is her recollection of "her native village, in Old England, and her paternal home; a decayed house of gray
stone, with a poverty-stricken aspect, but retaining a
half-obliterated shield of arms over the portal, in token
of antique gentility" [58]. *The Scarlet Letter* chronicles Hester's movement from a heraldry of the Old
World to a heraldry of the New—from a "token of
antique gentility" to a token better suited to symbolize
life in New England. Between the decaying home in
England and the stark gravestone in the wilderness is
a change from Old World to New that permeates the
entire book.

The nature of this change is made clear in the brief
first chapter of *The Scarlet Letter*. "The founders of a
new colony," writes Hawthorne, "whatever Utopia of
human virtue and happiness they might originally project, have invariably recognized it among their earliest
practical necessities to allot a portion of the virgin soil

127

as a cemetery, and another portion as the site of a prison" [47]. Idealism gives way to practicality. The contrast between idealism and grim practicality is picked up, in this chapter, in the contrast between the rosebush that grows beside the prison door and the prison itself, "the black flower of civilized society" [48]. This contrast is continued through the rest of the romance. Few readers of *The Scarlet Letter* miss the opposition in the book between scarlet and gray, between the passionate, feminine values associated with Hester and the severe, masculine values of the Puritan society.

It is important to note further, however, that Hawthorne associates the rosebush, Hester, the scarlet letter, and even Hester's needlework, not only with feminine passion or with a richer ideal of life but also (like roses in so many of his stories) with the values of the Old World as opposed to those of the New. Thus Hester, when she first appears, is not simply a woman of an "impulsive and passionate nature" [57]. Her magnificent clothes, noteworthy only because she is wearing them in Boston, are of the more lavish British fashion. She is specifically compared to a Catholic painting of the Virgin. Even her ornamentation of the scarlet letter is described as exemplifying a skill "of which the dames of a court might gladly have availed themselves") [81]. When Hester denies her passionate side in order to survive in the New World, it is important to note that it is also her European side that she is denying. The great moment in the forest when Hester lets down her hair and regains her passionate beauty

128

occurs only after she and Dimmesdale have determined to return to England. The "scarlet" side of Hester's character cannot survive in New England.

If Hester does pass on the qualities represented by the rosebush or the scarlet letter, it is through her daughter, Pearl. Hester deliberately represents, in the elaborate clothing she sews for Pearl, "the scarlet letter in another form" [102]. But the characteristics of Pearl are not transmitted to the character of New England in general. It is one of the curious features of *The Scarlet Letter* that Pearl, the only important character born in New England, is continually associated with Europe and eventually leaves New England to settle there. Pearl's association with the Old World is clear in the visit she and her mother pay to the mansion of Governor Bellingham—a scene in which Hawthorne is very much concerned with the tension in New England between the values of Old World and New. Bellingham's mansion clearly represents an attempt to reproduce in the New World the values of the Old. At the door Hester and Pearl are greeted by a servant who, we are told, "wore the blue coat, which was the customary garb of serving-men at that period, and long before, in the old hereditary halls of England." "Governor Bellingham," writes Hawthorne, "had planned his new habitation after the residences of gentlemen of fair estate in his native land" [104]. The costume of Bellingham himself, when he appears, is dominated by "the wide circumference of an elaborate ruff, beneath his gray beard, in the antiquated fashion of King James's reign" [108], recalling Hester's memory on the scaffold of "her father's face, with its bald brow, and reverend white beard, that flowed over the old-fashioned Elizabethan ruff" [58].

The garden, too, represents an attempt to transplant the values of the Old World. But here we see that such an attempt is doomed to failure. "The proprietor," we are told, "appeared already to have relinquished, as hopeless, the effort to perpetuate on this side of the Atlantic, in a hard soil and amid the close struggle for subsistence, the native English taste for ornamental gardening" [106]. Bellingham's attempt at an English garden is being overrun by pumpkins and cabbages. There are a few apple trees and rosebushes, but these, significantly, were planted by the Anglican Blackstone, the "flower-decked priest" of "The Maypole of Merry-Mount."[10] And, to return to my original point, it is with the roses, not the pumpkins, that Pearl identifies. She cries for a rose when she first sees the garden, and when the Reverend Mr. Wilson asks her who made her she "announced," so Hawthorne writes, "that she had not been made at all, but had been plucked by her mother off the bush of wild roses, that grew by the prison door" [112]. Pearl's association with Old England is not only symbolic. Bellingham, seeing her, is

[10] In Caleb Snow's *History of Boston* (Boston, 1828), which appears to have been Hawthorne's main source of historical background for *The Scarlet Letter*, Blackstone's gardening efforts are confined to "a garden plot and an orchard"; in fact, Snow writes that after leaving Boston Blackstone introduced apples into Rhode Island (p. 52). The roses, significantly, were added by Hawthorne. For the relation of *The Scarlet Letter* to Snow's *History* see Charles Ryskamp, "The New England Sources of *The Scarlet Letter*," *American Literature*, xxxi (1959), 257-72.

reminded of the court masks of the time of King James, of those called "the children of the Lord of Misrule" [109]. Wilson is reminded of stained-glass windows and pagan superstitions. "Methinks," he declares, "I have seen just such figures, when the sun has been shining through a richly painted window, and tracing out the golden and crimson images across the floor. But that was in the old land. . . . Art thou a Christian child,—ha? Dost know thy catechism? Or art thou one of those naughty elfs or fairies, whom we thought to have left behind us, with other relics of Papistry, in merry old England?" "I am mother's child," answers Pearl [109-10].

It might be objected that this picture of Pearl as European obscures the fact that she is the child of "nature," at home in the forest or on the seashore. To this I can only answer that for Hawthorne nature itself is more a part of the European character than of the American. "Nature" and the Old World are both comprehended, for Hawthorne, in the notion of the pagan— in the easy, permissive religion of "merry Old England" as opposed to the stern, repressive religion of New England. Thus in "The Maypole of Merry Mount" the forces of nature are represented, not by the Puritans but by the Anglican revelers. Hawthorne seems to have dissented from the popular belief that the proximity of the wilderness led to the growth of a "natural" American character. On the contrary, he seems to say, the first settlers were too close to nature to be "natural." "Nature" for them was not a rose garden but a wilderness, not a pastoral masque but an

Indian massacre. Both nature and Europe represented a threat to the stability of the new enterprise, and it is not always an easy matter to distinguish the part of each in the overall danger. Chillingworth has learned his black arts both from European scholars and wild Indians. It is almost indifferent to Hester, in considering escape from the restrictions of the Puritans, whether that escape be to the freedom of Europe or to the freedom of the wilderness.[11] And finally, to return to my original point, Pearl is at home both in the forest and in Europe.

The point is, with all due emphasis on the word "home," that Pearl is *not* at home in Boston. Her apparent disappearance to the continent at the close simply

---

[11] Edwin Fussell insists that the distinction between flight to Europe and flight to the forest is crucial, being symbolic of a choice betwen the "East" of the past and the "West" of the American future. (*Frontier: American Literature and the American West*, Princeton, 1965, pp. 92-95.) The idea suggests a rather different sort of "historical" concern in *The Scarlet Letter* (different, that is, from the concerns I am emphasizing), but I simply do not find anything in Hester's manner of considering the options of "East" and "West" to indicate that either she or Hawthorne thought the distinction between them (with reference to Hester's particular situation in Boston) to be of much importance. The main thing, it would seem, is to escape Boston. Professor Fussell also suggests an interpretation of Pearl quite different from my own association of Pearl with the European past. She is, he writes, "the Spirit of the West, the rising glory of America"; she is "America in person." (*Ibid.*, pp. 98, 105.) But I cannot see how this interpretation can accommodate the important fact that Pearl leaves America for Europe. According to Professor Fussell, Pearl remains in Europe "because, as the completely native and fully defined American, she is now free to go where she likes." (*Ibid.*, p. 113.) I would simply note, in reply, that Pearl is clearly *not* free to return to America—unless, like her mother, she drastically changes her character.

makes more explicitly the point made by the defeminiz-
ing of her mother—namely, that certain qualities of
richness and passion, both natural and European, did
not long survive the migration to New England. At the
beginning of the opening scene of *The Scarlet Letter*
Hawthorne comments on the changes that have taken
place in New England women since the time of the
first settlers:

> Morally, as well as materially, there was a coarser fibre in
> these wives and maidens of Old English birth and breed-
> ing, than in their fair descendants, separated from them
> by a series of six or seven generations; for, throughout that
> chain of ancestry, every successive mother has transmitted
> to her child a fainter bloom, a more delicate and briefer
> beauty, and a slighter physical frame, if not a character of
> less force and solidity, than her own. [50]

Pearl is no part of this historical progression toward a
"fainter bloom." Throughout all her character "there
was a trait of passion, a certain depth of hue, which
she never lost; and if, in any of her changes, she had
grown fainter or paler, she would have ceased to be
herself;—it would have been no longer Pearl!" [90].
As surely as the death of Ilbrahim in "The Gentle Boy"
the removal of Pearl at the end of *The Scarlet Letter*
signifies a narrowing or limitation of possibilities in the
growth of the American character. Hester must choose
at the close between Europe and America—between
living with her daughter abroad or returning to Boston.
She chooses the latter and her choice requires the sacrifice of a whole side of her character. As in "Endicott
and the Red Cross" or "The Maypole of Merry Mount"

133

so here, too, the price of independence is loss.[12] Even
on the scaffold, in the opening scene, Hester is aware
that she can never return to the Old World, that her
identity must now be adapted to the conditions of her
New World: her isolation, her child, the scarlet A on
her breast. "Yes!" we are told of her thoughts "—these
were her realities,—all else had vanished!" [59]. In
coming to terms with her "realities" Hester comes to
terms with the conditions of life in the wilderness. In
The Scarlet Letter (and one might speculate on further meanings for the initial A) Hester Prynne becomes, quite simply, an American.

The Young Minister: The Scarlet Letter

The Scarlet Letter opens in 1642 and closes (except
for the "Conclusion") in 1649.[13] Within this seven-
year time span several historical personages are intro-

---

[12] This same sort of loss is worked out even in the slightest
details. In the opening scene Hawthorne introduces a chorus of
four Puritan women, whose harshness is relieved by the kindness
and sympathy of a younger woman. During the final scene we are
told that "Hester saw and recognized the self-same faces of that
group of matrons, who had awaited her forthcoming from the
prison-door, seven years ago; all save one, the youngest and only
compassionate among them, whose burial-robe she had since made."
[246]

[13] Chapters XII to XXIII, from Dimmesdale's midnight vigil to
his final ascent of the scaffold, take place in 1649, since Winthrop's
death, which occurred in 1649, is mentioned prominently in Chapter XII. Since Pearl is seven years old in these chapters, and only
a few months old at the outset, the first scene of the romance,
from Chapter I through Chapter IV, is set seven years earlier—
that is, in 1642. Chapters VII and VIII, recounting the visit to
Bellingham's mansion, take place in 1645, since Pearl is three at
the time. (See Dawson, *Hawthorne's Knowledge and Use of New
England History*, p. 17.)

duced to represent different aspects of Puritan society. John Wilson, who had appeared in historical fiction as recently as Mrs. Lee's *Naomi* (1848), represents the Puritan clergy.[14] Richard Bellingham represents the civil authority of Boston. The selection of Bellingham is interesting because he is such a relatively minor historical figure next to, say, John Winthrop, whom Hawthorne could very easily have used at the beginning of his romance. In fact Winthrop, who succeeded Bellingham as governor on May 18, 1642, actually was in office at the time Hester is supposed to have been exposed on the scaffold. One might suggest any number of reasons to explain Hawthorne's use of Bellingham, rather than Winthrop, at the beginning of *The Scarlet Letter*. But one should also note that Hawthorne *does* use Winthrop later in the book. Although Winthrop never appears in person in *The Scarlet Letter*, his

---

[14] The use of Wilson, along with other aspects of the romance, suggests a rather intriguing line of speculation about the relation of the *plot* of *The Scarlet Letter*, and not just the background, to New England history. It is rather surprising that a work in which Wilson appears so frequently makes no mention whatever of John Cotton, Wilson's more famous colleague who was the mentor of Anne Hutchinson until forced to repudiate her in public. It is Dimmesdale, not Cotton, who is presented as Wilson's colleague. One wonders whether there may be more to the parallels between Dimmesdale and Cotton. Does the relationship between Dimmesdale and Hester Prynne, for instance, owe anything to Hawthorne's feelings about the relationship between Cotton and Anne Hutchinson? Hester is specifically compared to Anne Hutchinson, who is mentioned on the second page of the romance in connection with Hester's prison. In any case it is interesting to suppose that Dimmesdale's opening hypocritical questioning of Hester before the multitude has, somewhere in its background, Cotton's denunciation of his parishioner before the authorities of Massachusetts.

death, forming the background to Dimmesdale's midnight vigil on the scaffold, is conspicuous as the only actual historical *event* in the entire romance. Winthrop's death is more than a device for bringing various characters into the marketplace at midnight. Any death would have served this purpose. Hawthorne has even shifted dates—Winthrop died in March, Dimmesdale's vigil occurs in May—in order to make the event that brings the characters together not just any death, but specifically Winthrop's death.

As such it has a very special significance, since for Hawthorne and his contemporaries Winthrop was the founding father *par excellence*, the Washington of New England history. Winthrop was included in "Mrs. Hutchinson" in a tableau of "all those blessed fathers of the land, who rank in our veneration next to the evangelists of Holy Writ"; and also described there as "a man by whom the innocent and guilty might alike desire to be judged; the first confiding in his integrity and wisdom, the latter hoping in his mildness" [223]. The use of Bellingham rather than Winthrop at the beginning of *The Scarlet Letter* keeps Winthrop's reputation intact, permitting his death to retain its full symbolic impact. As the cowardly Dimmesdale chooses nighttime to "reveal" his secret sin, we are reminded repeatedly that the greatest of the founders, the representative of the generation of the fathers, has just passed away. The contrast between Dimmesdale and Winthrop, which is all to Winthrop's credit, is expressed in the A that appears in the sky during Dimmesdale's vigil. Dimmesdale takes this apparition as a symbol of his own adultery, while the townspeople interpret it as signifying the fact that Winthrop has just been made an angel. Most critics, following F. O. Matthiessen, see this ambiguity as an example of Hawthorne's use of the "device of multiple choice."[15] It is certainly at least that. But it is also more than that. The celestial A, with its two meanings, concentrates in a single symbol the contrast between the virtue of the old governor and the corruption of the young minister.

The great contrast between Dimmesdale and his elders is clear from the outset. Bellingham is "a gentleman advanced in years," Wilson is "the eldest clergyman of Boston" [64, 65]. Authority, in Boston, is based on age and strength. This was a community, Hawthorne writes, "which owed its origin and progress, . . . not to the impulses of youth, but to the stern and tempered energies of manhood, and the sombre sagacity of age" [64]. Dimmesdale is necessarily excluded from such a brotherhood; for the first thing we learn of him is that he is a "young clergyman" [66], and this epithet continues to be applied to him throughout the romance. Dimmesdale also lacks the manly strength of his elders. His eyes are "melancholy," his mouth "tremulous." "There was an air about this young minister,—an apprehensive, a startled, a half-frightened look,—as of a being who felt himself quite astray and at a loss in the pathway of human existence, and could only be at ease in some seclusion of his own" [66]. Dimmesdale's weakness, oddly, considering that he is

[15] F. O. Matthiessen, *American Renaissance*, New York, 1941, p. 276.

in the prime of life, continually distinguishes him from elders who are massive and powerful, even though they seem at the point of death in terms of age. It is fitting that Hester should demand of Dimmesdale, when they meet in the forest, "what hast thou to do with all these iron men, and their opinions?" [197]. Where they are strong he is weak, where they are firm he is "tremulous." And most inevitable for Dimmesdale, and important in terms of the frequency with which Hawthorne alludes to the fact, where they are old he is young.

Like Leonard Doane or Young Goodman Brown, Arthur Dimmesdale is a second-generation New England Puritan—at least by age and subordinate position if not by actual birth. In him the noble severity of the fathers has become morbid and enervated. But he is in many respects different from Leonard Doane or Goodman Brown. He neither ignores his own guilt nor, like these earlier characters, projects his sense of sin into a general conviction of total depravity. It is not Dimmesdale but Hester who is tempted to believe "that the outward guise of purity was but a lie" [86]. Furthermore, Dimmesdale does not reject the woman who offers him sympathy. Hester, to be sure, is not exactly a Faith Brown or a Mary Goffe. The extent of Dimmesdale's self-abasement, at the close, may smack of a kind of pride. But Dimmesdale's complete subordination of himself to Hester in the forest at least demonstrates that he is not guilty of the same sort of self-righteous pride that Goodman Brown brought back from *his* experience in the woods. Finally, one should note that

Dimmesdale does not represent the generation that succeeded the founding fathers for the simple reason that
most of the fathers succeed *him*. No more than Pearl
can Dimmesdale be seen as representing the future of
New England since, like Pearl though for different reasons, he does not remain in New England to take part
in that future. Why then, one wonders, has Hawthorne
gone to so much trouble to distinguish Dimmesdale
from his elders—to establish his youth and squeamish-
ness in the context of the age and strength of the
fathers, against the background of the death of Governor Winthrop? Dimmesdale seems to be part of some
historical formulation, but it is not absolutely clear just
what that formulation is.

These problems come to the surface again in the
last great scene of the romance, beginning with the
celebrations before the Election Sermon and ending
with Dimmesdale's death on the scaffold. Hawthorne
begins this sequence with a long discussion of Puritan
manners, whose purpose it is to demonstrate that the
Puritan fathers enjoyed the good life. He writes of the
Election celebration that the first settlers "would compare favorably, in point of holiday keeping, with their
descendants, even at so long an interval as ourselves"
[232]. "Their immediate posterity," he continues, inter-
jecting the note of decline from fathers to sons, "the
generation next to the early emigrants, wore the black-
est shade of Puritanism, and so darkened the national
visage with it, that all the subsequent years have not
sufficed to clear it up" [232]. Dimmesdale is the only
person in *The Scarlet Letter* whose age would associ-

ate him with the "immediate posterity" of the first
settlers.

After describing the crowd in the marketplace, Hawthorne devotes himself to the procession of dignitaries
marching to the meeting house. The description of this
procession contains the greatest tribute in all of Hawthorne's writing to the nobility of the founders. First
comes the military escort, but its glory is immediately
eclipsed by the solid magnificence of the "men of civil
eminence" who follow them. "It was an age," Hawthorne writes, "when what we call talent had far less
consideration than now, but the massive materials
which produce stability and dignity of character a
great deal more" [237]. The accent is again on power
and age, and on the notion that manliness has declined
into "talent" since the days of the founders. "These
primitive statesmen," Hawthorne continues, ". . . had
fortitude and self-reliance, and, in time of difficulty or
peril, stood up for the welfare of the state like a line
of cliffs against a tempestuous tide" [238]. It is in this
context that Dimmesdale is introduced—in the procession quite literally succeeding the founding fathers.
Dimmesdale seems to have overcome his weakness.
But his is not the strength of the fathers; it is rather
the nervous energy of the ascetic, whose "strength,"
we are told, "seemed not of the body." "Men of uncommon intellect," Hawthorne continues, "who have grown
morbid, possess this occasional power of mighty effort,
into which they throw the life of many days, and then
are lifeless for as many more" [239]. While the founders, we have just been told, are "distinguished by a

ponderous sobriety, rather than activity of intellect,"
Dimmesdale is distinguished for "intellectual ability"
[238]. He is a man "of uncommon intellect" [238]. Before the Election Sermon Hawthorne once again firmly
establishes the sense of decline, the sense of contrast
between the noble fathers and the young minister.

The Election Sermon itself, introduced in this context, is positively puzzling. It may be important, however, that since Winthrop was still governor of Massachusetts when he died in 1649, Dimmesdale's sermon
commemorates, not simply the election of a new governor, but more significantly the choosing of a succes-
sor to Winthrop—the establishment of a new order to
succeed that of the founders. "To-day," Hester explains
to Pearl at the beginning of the celebration, "a new
man is beginning to rule over them; and so . . . they
make merry and rejoice; as if a good and golden year
were at length to pass over the poor old world!"
[229].[16] Many commentators have noted as paradoxi-
cal the fact that the Holy Spirit vouchsafes so grand a
sermon to so sinful a minister. Dimmesdale himself,
we are told, "wondered that Heaven should see fit to

---

[16] Actually, of course, John Winthrop was succeeded in 1649
not by any "new man," but by our old friend John Endicott, who
went on to dominate the government of Massachusetts until his
own death in 1665 (making him governor, for instance, at the time
of "The Gentle Boy"). But Hawthorne goes out of his way, considering that what he is presenting is an election celebration, not
to mention who has been elected. It is Dimmesdale's day—unless,
of course, one wishes to argue that the suppressed "truth" about
Endicott's succession is intended ironically to undercut the hopefulness of Hester and Dimmesdale, to prove that it is not Dimmesdale's day after all.

transmit the grand and solemn music of its oracles through so foul an organ-pipe as he" [225]. But it is surely preposterous to equate the energy behind the writing of this sermon with an influx of the Holy Spirit. Dimmesdale's "energy" is not so much holy as nervous, permitting the sort of "mighty effort" typical of "men of uncommon intellect, who have grown morbid" [239]. Another, more important point is that the sermon itself is hardly the stuff of religious devotion—or at least of the sort of religious devotion we would expect of Dimmesdale. It is certainly unrelated either to Dimmesdale's own trials or to his new resolution to confess his sins and die. Dimmesdale delivers to the gathered throng not a sermon on sin and penitence but what becomes to all intents and purposes a ranting political oration, a hymn to American progress. "As he drew towards the close," Hawthorne writes, "a spirit as of prophecy had come upon him, constraining him to its purpose as mightily as the old prophets of Israel were constrained; only with this difference, that, whereas the Jewish seers had denounced judgments and ruin on their country, it was his mission to foretell a high and glorious destiny for the newly gathered people of the Lord" [249].

And the crowd that greets Dimmesdale as he emerges from the meeting house seems less a seventeenth-century congregation than a nineteenth-century mob. He is greeted with a tremendous shout of approval. "There were human beings enough," Hawthorne writes, "and enough of highly wrought and symphonious feeling, to produce that more impressive sound than the organ-tones of the blast, or the thunder, or the roar of the sea; even that mighty swell of many voices, blended into one great voice by the universal impulse which makes likewise one great heart out of the many. Never, from the soil of New England, had gone up such a shout! Never, on New England soil, had stood the man so honored by his mortal brethren as the preacher!" [250]. Dimmesdale seems to have become, in the midst of his agony, not so much a saint as a democratic political hero.[17] What, one wonders, does all this have to do with sin and penitence? What has Dimmesdale's final resolve to confess and die to do with the rising glory of America, with the sermon's assertion of historical progress? Perhaps it is Hawthorne's intention to deflate or satirize the sentiments of the sermon, by placing them so inappropriately in Dimmesdale's mouth. Yet even this explanation, while it may be accurate, does not explain why Hawthorne introduced the progressive sentiments in the first place. What, one is left wondering, does the direction of history have to do with Dimmesdale's predicament?

The answer, I believe, is that history has a great deal to do with this predicament. Dimmesdale's prob-

[17] It has been pointed out to me that Dimmesdale's delivery of a hymn to American progress in the context of Winthrop's death might bear some relation to the fact that Daniel Webster's first great assertion of the glorious future of the Republic was delivered on the occasion of the deaths of Adams and Jefferson. Of course it is impossible to know if Hawthorne had Webster in mind in presenting Dimmesdale's moment of triumph. But the plausibility of the association suggests what is in any case obvious in the book itself—namely, that Dimmesdale is a "democratic" or "progressive" hero only in an ironic sense.

lem is not simply a matter of morality (not having dared to confess his sin) or of psychology (having repressed, by denying Pearl, his own passionate impulses). It is, above all, a matter of history. He is a young man in a world dominated by old men, a son in a community of fathers. For Hester Europe represents a certain style of life, and the decision to flee to Europe represents a plan to return to that life. For Dimmesdale the flight to Europe is not so much a journey *toward* anything as a flight *from* the domination of the patriarchs. The sermon—occasioned by the death of the greatest of the patriarchs—is penned under the influence of the decision to escape; and it, too, represents a rebellion against Dimmesdale's subordination, as a son, to the massive solidity of his elders. The sermon is a rebellion because in the face of decline it asserts progress; in the shadow of the fathers it asserts a movement away from that shadow into a more glorious future belonging to the sons. The horror of Dimmesdale's predicament is that there is no progress. He cannot reverse the tide of history, he can finally only attempt to escape it. Like Neal's George Burroughs or Dawes's Edward Fitzvassal, Hawthorne's Arthur Dimmesdale is trapped by the myth of the founding fathers. He dreams of escaping this trap but learns at the end that the only possible escape is death, the escape from all history.

Thus Dimmesdale's final moments, after his appeal to progress has been undercut by his returning bodily weakness, are devoted not just to confession and death, but to a concerted effort to flee the fathers. When "the venerable John Wilson" offers support to the enfeebled

young minister that minister, so we are told, "tremu-
lously, but decidedly, repelled the old man's arm"
[251]. Then Hawthorne includes a bit of description
which rather shockingly reveals the thoroughness with
which the minister has turned from the fathers.
Dimmesdale walks on with a movement, Hawthorne
writes, "which rather resembled the wavering effort of
an infant, with its mother's arms in view, outstretched
to tempt him forward" [251]. As Dimmesdale approaches Hester, the maternal alternative to the Puritan authorities, Bellingham steps forward to assist him.
"But there was something in the [minister's] expression," we are told, "that warned back the magistrate"
[252]. Dimmesdale holds out his arms to Hester, but
there is yet another old man in the crowd. "At this in-
stant," writes Hawthorne, "old Roger Chillingworth
thrust himself through the crowd . . . to snatch back
his victim from what he sought to do!" "The old man,"
Hawthorne continues, "rushed forward and caught the
minister by the arm" [252]. But as he rejects the Puritan fathers, so Dimmesdale rejects this old man whose
"love" for the "young pastor" was earlier described as
"paternal" [125]. "Come hither now," Dimmesdale
cries to Hester, "and twine thy strength about me! . . .
This wretched and wronged old man is opposing it
with all his might! . . . Come, Hester, come! Support
me up yonder scaffold!" [253]. As in the forest, so
here, Dimmesdale's escape from the fathers is tied to
the strength of Hester.

Of course there is a difference between the Dimmesdale of the forest and the Dimmesdale of the scaffold.

In the forest he had submitted himself completely to Hester's strength and direction. On the scaffold he still relies on her strength, but he himself is now making the decisions. To the cry of "Thy strength, Hester," he adds; "but let it be guided by the will which God hath granted me!" [253]. Dimmesdale is finally turning from denial—of Hester and of Pearl—to control, both literally and symbolically. And there is something heroic in this final act of the hitherto squeamish minister. Still, it would be a mistake to overstate the case for Dimmesdale's heroism, as some critics have done, especially at the expense of Hester's stature at the end.[18] Dimmesdale's escape may be grand and it may even be tragic, but it is an escape all the same. Hester must remain to bear the burden of history. Hester endures, returning voluntarily to live out her days in Boston. It is she who provides the continuity between past and present. For of all the major characters who attempt to find a home in this wilderness only Hester succeeds. "There was more real life for Hester Prynne," Hawthorne writes, "here, in New England, than in that unknown region where Pearl had found a home" [262-63]. Only Hester is able to make the sacrifice, the adaptations, necessary for survival in New England. It is to Hester then—and to a few other heroines in the fiction of Hawthorne and his contemporaries—that I turn in the next chapter.

[18] For instance Professor Male writes that "where Hester's ascension was limited, [Dimmesdale's] is complete." (*Hawthorne's Tragic Vision*, p. 98.)

CHAPTER FOUR

FATHERS AND DAUGHTERS

normally happens is that a young man wants a young woman, that his desire is resisted by some opposition, usually paternal, and that near the end of the play some twist in the plot enables the hero to have his will." "The movement of comedy," he continues, "is usually a movement from one kind of society to another. At the beginning of the play the obstructing characters are in charge of the play's society. . . . At the end of the play the device in the plot that brings hero and heroine together causes a new society to crystallize around the hero, and the moment when this crystallization occurs is the point of resolution in the action, the comic discovery."[1] I think we can see that a plot formula which represents and celebrates the transformation from an old society to a new is admirably suited to exemplifying a progressive notion of history. In fact, I would contend that one cannot understand these books at all without understanding how the "comic" or "romantic" marriage plot is often a book's principal expression of its author's attitude toward history.

Obstructing Figures: The Father and the Villain

According to Professor Frye, "comedy often turns on a clash between a son's and a father's will."[2] The father's opposition to the marriage of hero and heroine is frequently, in historical romance, one of the principal obstacles to comic resolution—as well as one of the principal manifestations of the old society. In the terms

[1] Northrop Frye, *The Anatomy of Criticism*, Princeton, N.J., 1957, p. 163.
[2] *Ibid.*, p. 164.

of the romantic historians, one would say that the obstructive authority of the father represents the "tyranny" of the past. Thus the intolerance of the Puritan society in Mrs. Child's *Hobomok*—its banishing of Episcopalians—is realized in the plot in Mr. Conant's refusal to allow his daughter to marry an Episcopalian. There are exceptions to the association of the father or paternal figure with tyranny, but they *are* exceptions. For the most part the Puritan father is harsh, bigoted, and intolerant in both his public and his private relations—in both the Puritan community and the world of the romantic marriage plot.

A rather mild example of the convention is the marriage plot in Mrs. Cheney's *A Peep at the Pilgrims*. Edward Atherton, an Episcopalian visitor to Plymouth, falls in love with Miriam Grey, a Puritan girl. Their romance is strongly opposed by Miriam's father on strictly sectarian grounds. "My religion and my principles are more precious to me," he announces, "than the gratification of any worldly feelings, the enjoyment of any temporal pleasure;—even than the earthly happiness of my child" [168]. How far Mr. Grey is willing to ignore the "earthly happiness" of his daughter can be seen in his encouragement of the attentions of the "sanctimonious Benjamin Ashley," the ridiculous hypocrite, simply because Ashley observes the forms of Puritanism. A young friend of Atherton's, in a letter, puts his finger on the symbolic political significance of Mr. Grey's actions. "I well know," he writes, "it is all owing to that grim father of hers that you and Miriam are separated. . . . I wonder wherein was the use of people's coming over to this savage wilderness, for the sake of liberty of conscience, as they call it, if they will not allow any one to think differently from themselves, now they are here, nor to marry whom they choose, and be happy if they can" [II, 128]. The unnatural intolerance of the Puritans is fully represented in the sectarian refusal of the father to permit the natural marriage of hero and heroine. Of course the young people finally prevail. After Atherton saves Miriam from Indian captivity, Mr. Grey gives in, and the hero and heroine are married. Atherton eventually becomes a Puritan, although we are told pointedly that this Puritan is "liberal" [II, 275]. The cross-sectarian marriage of the children represents a distillation of the harsh Puritanism of the fathers. The artificiality of sectarianism gives way to the naturalness of tolerance.

Again and again these historical romances recapitulate the conventional opposition of paternal repression and filial natural instinct. This opposition is obviously to a large extent psychological. In *Naomi*, for example, the heroine clearly represents the heart as against the head—as against the subtle, intellectual perversions of Puritanism.[3] But this opposition is historical as well as psychological in its meaning; it implies an historical movement from one psychological condition to another—from a society dominated by the head to a society liberated by the heart. This movement is clear,

[3] It has seemed wise to use psychological terms like "heart" and "head" (as opposed to their modern approximates, "id" and "ego") for the simple reason that these are the words used by the authors we are considering.

to cite one more example, in Paulding's *The Puritan and His Daughter*—the very title of which is an embodiment of the opposition under discussion. In this book the marriage of the Puritan, Miriam Habingdon, to the Episcopalian, Langley Tyringham, is prohibited by both their fathers—the one a dour Puritan, the other a Cavalier. The normal symbolic overtones of the conventional romantic plot are quite clear. Miriam, we learn, "was naturally full of poetic feeling; but both the precepts and example of her father had taught her to limit her enthusiasm to piety alone" [I, 146]. Her romance with Langley releases some of the "poetic feeling" suppressed by her father. Langley, meanwhile, provides the appropriate symbolic reading of the parental prohibition. "How can those," he reasons with himself, "that like my father, who, though loyal to his sovereign, has learned in this new world of unrestricted reason to scorn the slavish doctrine of passive obedience and non-resistance—how can they deny the application of this principle to a tyrant king, and apply it to a tyrant father!" Domestic tyranny is again representative of political and religious tyranny. "Is it for the father," Langley continues, "to command at will, and the son to obey against the impulses of his heart, and the convictions of his understanding?" [I, 197].

The answer, of course, is "No"; Langley and Miriam are finally married, and Paulding gives this marriage its appropriate symbolic dimension. "Those feelings of religious and political antipathy," he writes, "which had alienated their fathers, and caused so much suffering to their children, did not take root in the soil of mutual love. . . . America—we mean the United States, the legitimate representative of the New World—is not the soil or genial clime for bigotry and persecution" [II, 267-68]. Thus in the conventional portrayal of the movement from intolerance to liberty the father is doubly conventional. As narrow Puritan he represents a conventional attitude toward history. As obstructing figure he represents an element of fictional convention. It is impossible to understand conventional historical romance without understanding the way in which, over and over again, it fuses these two kinds of convention, historical and literary.

PATERNAL AUTHORITY is not the only obstacle in the the way of the final marriage. The heroine is also often confronted by a villain who attempts to seduce her from the path of progress. The seduction plot, pitting lascivious villain against virtuous heroine, is not derived from Greek New Comedy. While the theme of seduction is no doubt as old as the act from which it derives, it descends—for the authors of the earlier nineteenth century—either directly or indirectly from the two great seduction novels of Samuel Richardson, *Pamela* and *Clarissa*. But the villain was easily adapted to the purposes of the comic marriage plot as yet another obstruction in the way of the movement toward marriage and comic resolution.

According to Leslie Fiedler the sexual battle between virtuous heroine and depraved villain was at least in part intended, in European fiction, as a vindication of the rising middle class as against the still-powerful aristocracy. "Part of the appeal of the seduction novel," he writes, "rested surely on its presentation of the conflict of aristocracy and bourgeoisie within the confines of the boudoir."[4] It is often asserted that American literature substitutes abstract oppositions for the social distinctions found in English novels but lacking in American life. In any case it is certainly true of the books under discussion that the social opposition between upper and lower classes is replaced by a more abstract contest. In these books the heroine's struggle with the villain represents, not the social struggle between bourgeoisie and aristocracy, but rather the symbolic political struggle between liberty and tyranny that romantic historians liked to see as the "principle" of American history. In many of these books sex and politics become metaphorically interchangeable. For example, a character in *Nix's Mate* exclaims, "The man who submits to the least infringement of his rights, without putting a stop to such infringements peremptorily . . . is situated precisely like a woman who has not checked the advances of licentiousness" [i, 122-23]. The villain is associated, not with a different social class, but with the abstract force of tyranny and arbitrary authority. He is often literally associated with paternal authority, having managed to deceive the fathers with respect to his true intentions. In one extreme case the villain *is* authority: in Herbert's *The*

---

[4] Leslie A. Fiedler, *Love and Death in the American Novel*, New York, 1960, p. 40.

Fair Puritan the virtue of the title figure is attacked by no less than the royal governor, Andross (whose name Herbert misspells throughout).

The seducing villain can be, and often is, a narrow Puritan. In a sense Benjamin Ashley, whose favor with Mr. Grey threatens the love of hero and heroine in *A Peep at the Pilgrims*, functions as a villain. But the really villainous Puritans—those pursuing not marriage but the heroine's "virtue"—invariably appear in association with the witchcraft persecutions. It is interesting to see how, in these books, the act of attempted seduction is linked with intolerance. Toward the end of Paulding's *The Puritan and His Daughter*, for example, Miriam Habingdon and her father move to a frontier settlement in Massachusetts. Before long, Miriam's father dies, and the hypocrite Tobias Harpsfield tries to marry her for her money. When Miriam rejects him he vows vengeance and has her accused and convicted of witchcraft. Fortunately, Miriam is rescued at the last minute by the hero, Langley Tyringham. This pattern of proposal, refusal, and accusation is important because it occurs in some form in several of these books—including *The Spectre of the Forest*, *Mercy Disborough*, and *The Salem Belle*. A comic version of the same pattern provides the main plot of the early satire of Puritanism, *Salem Witchcraft*. All this has led one critic to complain that most of these writers, incapable of understanding the real motives of those who accused others of being witches, ignored the actual events and motives of 1692 and resorted instead "to fairly simple patterns of malice or jealousy. . . . It was this inherent plot weakness that accounts for the constant recurrence of fair Puritans charged with witchcraft."[5] Here we have a specific instance in which writers invariably chose the conventional over the historical. But what matters about their attribution of witchcraft to sexual jealousy is not that it falsifies the historical record so much as that it reveals once again how these authors used fictional conventions to elaborate the central conflict they saw in all American history—the conflict between liberty and tyranny. In this view of New England history the witchcraft crisis becomes simply the last desperate (and unsuccessful) effort of the forces of tyranny to subordinate or exterminate liberty once and for all.

These romances also abound with non-Puritan villains. And although Catholicism is not always treated with hostility, for the most part these non-Puritan villains are Catholics. In the anonymous *Panola; or, The Indian Sisters* (1849), a lascivious French Canadian named Tom Maule repeatedly attempts to seduce the daughter of a Puritan minister. The villainous Governor Andross, in Herbert's *The Fair Puritan*, is presented as a Catholic. Most villainous of them all is an historical New England Catholic, Sir Christopher Gardiner, who appears as villain in two of these romances—Motley's *Merry-Mount* and Catharine Maria Sedgwick's *Hope Leslie* (as Sir *Philip* Gardiner).[6] In

[5] G. Harrison Orians, "New England Witchcraft in Fiction," *American Literature*, II (1930), 71.

[6] See Bradford Torrey Schantz, "Sir Christopher Gardiner in Nineteenth Century American Fiction," *New England Quarterly*, XI (1938), 807-17. Gardiner appears briefly as the misunder-

Motley's romance Gardiner is so completely the literary villain that he threatens to become a parody of the type. He is provided with a background that includes three seductions, political intrigue, and an almost successful effort to be elected to the Papacy. In America he is secretly scheming to wrest New England from the Puritans and deliver it to his patron, Sir Ferdinando Gorges. We do not need to get involved in the formidable plot of *Merry-Mount*. Suffice it to say that toward the end of the book Gardiner kidnaps the heroine, Esther Ludlow, and takes her off, as they say, to the woods, where he gives her six hours to decide between being married and being raped. Needless to say, the hero appears in the nick of time, Gardiner is banished, and the hero and heroine are married.

But during Esther's captivity it is quite clear that the struggle between heroine and villain involves more than the threatened loss of Esther's virginity. It is no coincidence that Gardiner is also involved in Catholic schemes for the control of the territory of New England. The Catholic villain is always linked, in his attempt on the virginity of the heroine, with the attempts of the forces of European tyranny to conquer and possess the virgin New World. Thus when Gardiner is refused, he threatens Esther in the language of political tyranny: "Then live to be my hand-maid, my bond-

---

stood sentimental hero of an inset tale in Whittier's *Leaves from Margaret Smith's Journal*. He also appears as the hero of John Turvill Adams's *Knight of the Golden Melice* (1857) and in Longfellow's "Rhyme of Sir Christopher," the Landlord's Tale in *Tales of a Wayside Inn* (1873).

woman, my slave!" [II, 209]. At the same time that he is assuring Esther, "You are at this moment irrevocably within my power," he is also claiming, "The whole rich province of Massachusetts is, at this moment, a manor, belonging to me alone" [II, 209, 207]. Esther's rejection of Gardiner's advances represents the force of freedom, the force that resists tyranny. Gardiner's defeat represents a symbolic step forward in the glorious progress from tyranny to liberty—from, in this case, *European* tyranny to *American* liberty.

The Rebellious Daughter

But the great theme of the historical romance of New England was not the conflict between Puritanism and external tyranny but the conflict within Puritanism itself between the forces of tyranny and the forces of liberty. Thus the figure of the European villain, representing the threat of external tyranny, is not nearly as important in this literature as the figure of the Puritan tyrant—the jealous Puritan villain, and especially the repressive Puritan father. In almost every one of these books the hero and heroine are of different religious denominations, so that the final marriage, overcoming the artificial distinctions of the fathers, signifies the dawning of a new, liberated age. "Like the bird that spreads his wings, and soars above the limits by which each man fences his own narrow domains," writes Catharine Sedgwick of her heroine in *Hope Leslie*, "[Hope] enjoyed the capacities of her nature, and permitted her mind to expand beyond the contracted boundaries of sectarian faith" [I, 180]. The

159

great historical contest between freedom and repression finds fictional embodiment in the conventional comic contest between children and their fathers.

A particular feature of this comic contest, as presented in the historical romance of New England, deserves closer attention. According to Professor Frye, "comedy often turns on a clash between a son's and a father's will."[7] Yet again and again in these books the antagonist of the father is not the son, but the daughter. The conventional role of the hero is almost always subordinate to that of the heroine. Although there are important exceptions, it is generally true that the hero does not, himself, initiate the subversion of paternal authority. Again and again he accepts his subordinate position by accepting without reservation the values of the heroine. His subordination often takes the form of a religious conversion to the natural religion of the heroine. She, in disagreeing with the intolerance of the fathers, establishes the basis of the new society. The hero becomes part of the new society, not by rebelling himself, but by accepting the heroine's values.

One cannot help speculating on the reasons for the importance of the heroine in this fiction.[8] It would be

[7] Frye, *The Anatomy of Criticism*, p. 164.

[8] These romances are hardly unique in giving such importance to the heroine. One thinks, for example, of the heroines of Shakespearean comedy (or of Cordelia), to which many of these authors are undoubtedly at least partially indebted for their portraits of women. One might think of Spenser's Una or Britomart, or of the Lady in Milton's *Comus*. One surely thinks of the more nearly contemporary heroines of Richardson and his imitators, or of Jane Austen. What matters here, however, is not literary influence, but simply the fact of the heroine's great importance in the books being discussed.

easy to attribute this importance to the number of women writing at the time. But the same sort of heroine appears in works written by men; even Paulding wrote his romance of seventeenth-century New England about a Puritan and his *daughter*. One could cite the great proportion of women in the reading public, and these writers were undoubtedly aware of their audience. But a more significant factor behind the importance of the heroine would seem to lie in the peculiar symbolic advantages of the *female* rebel against authority. The unfortunate connotations and consequences of male rebellion are clear in *Nix's Mate* and *Rachel Dyer*. In *Nix's Mate* rebellion is equated with parricide. The male rebel, apparently, is aiming too deliberately at the overthrow of the father for his protest to go unpunished. Both Edward Fitzvassal and George Burroughs are executed by those in authority. The female rebel, on the other hand, avoids overt revolution. However wrong-headed she may feel her father to be, she never disobeys him. For instance Paulding tells us that Miriam Habingdon found her father's "restrictions unreasonable." "Still," he adds, "she offered no objection, but as usual acquiesced in his wishes with silent resignation. She was obedient, as well from a habit of duty, as from the dictates of conscience" [II, 44]. For the most part these heroines are more reluctant even than Richardson's Clarissa to disobey an erring father. Yet the heroine's obedience serves, curiously, to make her an effective rebel where a young man is doomed to failure. Her revolt is, as we shall see, primarily symbolic—her very nature brings about the transformation of society. Since her rebellion is not a matter of action, she can escape responsibility for it. She can, in fact, be held up as an exemplar of obedience. Thus only the young woman can be opposed to the fathers with impunity; only she can safely be the champion of the new society.

It is thus extremely interesting to survey the characteristics of the heroines of these books. Some of these characteristics have already been encountered, especially in the feminine good sense and natural piety of Mrs. Lee's Naomi Worthington. The heroine embodies the characteristics associated with the "heart" as opposed to the "head." As she avoids the Puritan perversion of the heart's simple truths, so her religion is free of those errors of intellectual subtlety and un-Christian intolerance exhibited by the Puritans. "There is no tendency in your religion," says the hero to the heroine in *The Salem Belle*, "to blend itself with superstition" [83]. But however serious her religion, the heroine is never herself morbid. Mrs. Lee relates that a lonely childhood might have turned Naomi into a fanatic or a "superstitious devotee." "But fortunately," she continues, "nature had endowed her with a vigorous reason, a strong good-sense, that prevented her from becoming either the one or the other" [41]. In fact, so far is the conventional heroine from morbidity that gaiety (albeit "modest" gaiety) is very often one of her most important characteristics. Miriam Grey, in Mrs. Cheney's *A Peep at the Pilgrims*, affects a rather harmless cap of ribbons until ordered to remove it by her father. "It is too, too gay," announces Mr. Grey

162

(whose name is surely not without meaning). "I would not see you, my child decked out in garlands" [I, 100].[9] Herbert's Ruth Whalley is subjected to her father's "cold domestic tyranny" "because she was, what the good God intended that we all should be, joyous herself, and a minister of joy to others" [25, 27]. We are told of her father, significantly, that "smiles were strangers to his gloomy nature" [37].

Again and again the heroine's gay natural spirits are brought out through their opposition to the severity of those "forefathers" who, in the words of Mrs. Lee, "never seriously considered the consequences of stopping up the spout of the tea-kettle" [*Naomi*, 151]. "Whatever gratified the natural desires of the heart," writes Catharine Sedgwick of the Puritans in *Hope Leslie*, "was questionable, and almost everything that was difficult and painful assumed the form of duty" [I, 230]. Miriam Habingdon's father, according to Paulding, "checked the vivacity of [his daughter's] youth, and was intolerant of all those little amusements, or recreations that had for their object merely whiling away the hour" [II, 44]. The symbolism implicit in the natural heroine is even clearer in the fascinating description that introduces the title character of William Leete Stone's *Mercy Disborough*:

Her mouth was delicately formed, and her whole countenance lighted up with large mild eyes, beaming like twin

[9] The linking of Puritan intolerance with the attack on gay clothing undoubtedly owes something to Nathaniel Ward's *The Simple Cobbler of Aggawam* (1647), an exuberant attack on toleration in which is included an attack on women's fashions.

orbs of living blue. The austere manners of the day, which imposed restraints upon the natural vivacity of the sex, had imparted a tinge to the expression of her features, not exactly of severity, nor of melancholy, though perhaps a little of both; but Mercy could smile as sweetly as any maiden in the colony. . . . Her hair was dark brown, bordering upon the auburn; but in obedience to the rigid custom of the times, no curls or ringlets were allowed to stray over her well-arched temples; although the thick glossy tresses which fell in profusion upon her neck and shoulders would sometimes wickedly rebel, as they played lightly in the wanton breeze. Her spirits were naturally buoyant, while the disposition of Naomi was not more sweetly submissive, nor that of Ruth more confiding. [8]

The entire description is structured on the opposition of artificial constraint and natural good spirits. And the conjunction of this hair, which "wickedly rebels" in the "wanton" breeze, with Mercy's "sweetly submissive" disposition shows just how it is that the heroine can overthrow the fathers without doing so deliberately. She does not defy the fathers openly; she is thoroughly obedient. Her rebellion, rather, is symbolic. It is the inevitable result of association with the forces of nature, of the heart. It is through no fault of the heroine, but only as a result of the nature of things, that these characteristic qualities are unalterably opposed to the unnatural restrictions imposed by the head.

The character of the natural heroine is probably most fully developed in Catharine Maria Sedgwick's *Hope Leslie*.[10] Hope Leslie's naturalness is brought out

---

[10] For a fuller discussion of *Hope Leslie* see my article, "History and Romance Convention in Catharine Sedgwick's *Hope Leslie*," *American Quarterly*, XXII (1970), 213-21.

by contrast with a pious, subservient friend named Esther Downing. Esther is described as "a godly, gracious maiden . . . approved by [her] elders." "She attained the age of nineteen," we are told, "without one truant wish straying beyond the narrow bound of domestic duty and religious exercises" [i, 194, 198]. Esther reveals her narrowness by protesting to the heroine: "you do allow yourself too much liberty of thought and word: you certainly know that we owe implicit deference to our elders and superiors; we ought to be guided by their advice, and governed by their authority." Hope, however, has a rather more liberal notion of her "duty." "As to authority," she replies, "I would not be a machine to be moved at the pleasure of anybody that happened to be a little older than myself" [i, 262]. Hope is not openly defiant, but she follows the dictates of her heart when they conflict with the dictates of her elders. And she is thoroughly natural. Her fashion-conscious aunt writes in a letter that she (the aunt) did not believe the color of a new dress to be *feuille morte*. "Hope," she writes, "thought to convince me I was wrong by matching it with a dead leaf from the forest. Was not that peculiar of Hope?" [i, 170]. Even as a physical attribute Hope's naturalness is opposed to tyranny. "Fashion," we are told, "had no shrines among the Pilgrims: but where she is most abjectly worshipped, it would be treason against the paramount right of Nature to subject such a figure as Hope Leslie's to her tyranny" [i, 177].

This opposition of nature and constraint can also be seen in many descriptions of external nature in these books. It emerges, for instance, in *Mercy Disborough*, in the description of a day of silent prayer and humiliation during which the animals are tethered outside the church. "The reigning silence," we are told, "was deep and profound, save when broken by the impatient neighings of the famishing horses, and the lowings and bleatings of the flocks and herds, doomed, for the sins of man, to suffer a penance which they could not understand" [33]. One might compare to this the account of the rise of the witchcraft crisis in *The Salem Belle*:

The [Sabbath] day was singularly beautiful; the freshness of its early dawning, and the summer breezes, that were diffusing life and joyousness around, were expressive of a mild and beneficent Providence; but Nature in her calm and delightful aspect, was all unconscious of the dark figures and mysterious demons, that were thronging the imaginations of men; her morning hymn was ascending in grateful chorus from forest, valley, and stream; but she was no longer the handmaid of devotion, for man refused to mingle in her silent or audible aspirations, or in any sense, to bend the knee at her shrine. [123-24]

This nature, "diffusing life and joyousness around," performs the same function as the conventional heroine, the function of standing in opposition to the severity of the fathers. The heroine in these books is often symbolically interchangeable with nature—at least with this particular nature, "in her calm and delightful aspect."

According to Perry Miller the literary idea of "Romance" signified, "for Scott and his adulators," "Nature with a capital N—Nature as meaning both universal human nature and natural landscape."[11] Again and again these romances tell us to trust nature, to trust the heart—the psychological equivalent of the "natural." But the heroine, and the "joyous" nature associated with her, reveal just how circumscribed was the conventional ideal of the "natural"—psychological or external—linked with "Romance." It does not seem to have occurred to these writers that the heart (at least the heroine's heart) was anything but the joyous abode of sunshine. We are constantly being offered the untroubled, feminine, natural heart as the solution to all the problems of a troubled, masculine, unnatural world. It is seldom mentioned that there are immodest as well as modest forms of gaiety, or that the heroine's heart may have its own excesses. We are expected in *Naomi*, for example, to sympathize completely with a basically solipsistic girl who dismisses all the wisdom of her elders simply because it contradicts the dictates of her heart. To be sure, Mrs. Lee finds it necessary to absolve her heroine of the charge of egotism or spiritual pride. But she *does* absolve her. Naomi remains to the end the redeeming symbol of truth in a world dominated by error.

The heroine's function is ethical as well as symbolic, which is why, I suspect, modern readers find her so objectionable. To set up a "natural" heroine as a foil to Puritan intolerance is one thing. As foil the heroine represents an ideal of the natural as against the actu-

[11] Perry Miller, "The Romance and the Novel," *Nature's Nation*, Cambridge, Mass., 1967, p. 247.

ality of the unnatural. The point of the contrast is to emphasize the discrepancy between actual and ideal. As an ethical norm, however, the heroine has the function of obscuring or denying this discrepancy, of assuring us that it doesn't matter. She stands for the literally *simple*-minded belief (or desire to believe) that all problems and complexities are but clouds artificially covering the "fair simplicity" of essential truth. Most critics see this conventional heroine as a prudish, "Victorian" denial of female sexuality; and she is certainly that. She simplifies sex because she denies, by being both "pure" and "wanton," the real complexity of sexuality—the potential discrepancy between the ideal and the actual.

In the historical romance of New England this heroine has an at least equally important function of obscuring, rather than clarifying, the problems raised by the early history of the region. For there is a great discrepancy between the ideal of the migration and the actuality of the settlement—between the notion that the founders came here for liberty of conscience and the fact that they arrived only to establish a new form of tyranny. As foil the heroine quite properly emphasizes this problem—indicating just how far the fathers have gone in abandoning their trust. But by remaining the dutiful daughter to the end, and by being rewarded at that end, the natural heroine allows these writers, as it were, to have their cake and eat it too. Like the heroines they are portraying, these writers can affirm the new society without repudiating the old. The fathers are most often included in the comic ending, and while this may be good comedy, it is rather unconvincing history. At the close of *A Peep at the Pilgrims*, for instance, Mrs. Cheney writes of Mr. Grey, who had staunchly opposed the marriage of hero and heroine, that he "lived to enjoy a green old age, and saw a new generation rising up to take the place of their fathers, and hand down to their children's children those principles of civil and religious freedom, which guided the Pilgrims to the rock of Plymouth" [II, 276]. This is all very well, but how are we to reconcile these "principles of civil and religious freedom" with the intolerant practice of Mr. Grey and his friends throughout the book? The problem with *A Peep at the Pilgrims* is that this question is hardly even asked, let alone answered. We are simply expected to accept the magical transformation of Mr. Grey from intolerance to tolerance. What is more important, since it extends the demands of comedy into the analysis of history, is that we are also asked to accept the idea that the "principles" of toleration have guided Mr. Grey all along. In this case literary convention is *substituted* for historical analysis. The heroine and the final marriage assert fictional progress in the face of what, historically, could only be regarded as deterioration—as the betrayal of the promise of freedom in America. It is no doubt significant that there is no heroine as such in the one book unflinchingly to assert decline, Cooper's *The Wept of Wish-Ton-Wish*.

It would be something of an exaggeration to say that the natural heroine, the "rebellious daughter," has no basis in seventeenth-century history. Puritan New England had a small but genuine tradition of feminine dissent. All the same, the natural heroine is much more significantly a product of certain nineteenth-century yearnings toward simplicity, a reaction against the realities and complexities of either century. Yet for all the oversimplification of life which she represents, we should not ignore this heroine. She was extremely important for Hawthorne's contemporaries. And Hawthorne himself was profoundly influenced by this character type. To understand Hawthorne's relation to his more conventional contemporaries, we must understand the importance to them of their conventions. We should note, for instance, the reading which one character in *Hope Leslie* gives to the heroine's natural self-assurance—her desire, as he puts it, to have her own way. "This having our own way," he announces, "is what everybody likes; it's the privilege we came to this wilderness world for." "Times are changed—" the character continues, "there is a new spirit in the world—chains are broken—fetters are knocked off—and the liberty set forth in the blessed Word is now felt to be every man's birth right" [II, 68]. All this is derived from "this having one's own way." Hope Leslie's "spirit," in short, is the "spirit" of democracy, of American history. It is important to realize how completely, here and elsewhere, the conventional heroine is used as a political symbol. She represents not so much qualities as forces (as Henry Adams would see in his own way)—not so much innocence, for example, as "liberty." Hope Leslie *is* liberty, she *is* progress. In her character, and in the character of the other conventional heroines of this literature, the historical romancers found what they were looking for—the romantic "principle" behind the events of the seventeenth century in New England.

BEHIND MOST OF these romances is the same essential plot, the romantic marriage plot celebrating the victory of the natural daughter over her repressive father. The psychological connotations of a convention which pits emotion against intellect and children against parents ought to be clear. We must be aware of how important the psychological ideas of these authors are to their treatment of New England history. It is interesting in this light that in his provocative recent examination of Hawthorne's psychological themes Frederick Crews has argued that Hawthorne's concern with New England history is primarily a projection of Hawthorne's personal psychological concerns—that "Hawthorne's interest in history is only a special case of his interest in fathers and sons, guilt and retribution . . . ; the history of the nation interests him *only* as it is metaphorical of individual mental strife."[12] Professor Crews's book is of great value in showing the parallels, in Hawthorne's historical fiction, between psychological and historical patterns of repression and liberation. These parallels are important even if we reject the corollary that "for Hawthorne . . . the sense of the past

[12] Frederick Crews, *The Sins of the Fathers: Hawthorne's Psychological Themes*, New York, 1966, pp. 28-29.

is nothing other than the sense of symbolic family conflict writ large."[13] The symbolic family conflict is there, but it is not the only thing that is there, for the simple reason that parallels or analogies necessarily work both ways. If Hawthorne uses history to comment on psychology, he also uses psychology to comment on history.

Hawthorne is by no means unique in viewing history through psychology, nor does he even rely so much as many of his contemporaries on the assumption of a congruence of historical and psychological patterns of liberation. The essence of the conventional marriage plot is, after all, "symbolic family conflict writ large." It is extremely important that we understand how extensively almost all the historical romancers of New England rely on the psychology of heart and head for an understanding of the nature and direction of history. The rebellion of heart against head is linked, in romance after romance, with the rebellion of children against their fathers. The question of whether or not this rebellion is "Oedipal" strikes me as being finally rather silly. All of these writers have lain too long in the grave to be transferred to the couch without damage. What really matters, it seems to me, is that we note how psychological pattern becomes political myth in these books—and that we note how both are linked, in book after book, with the conventional marriage plot, whose essence also is the conflict between fathers and children. Above all, it is the interpenetration of these psychological, literary, and historical patterns of

[13] *Ibid.*, p. 60.

repression and liberation that makes the historical romance of New England interesting to the modern
reader. It is this complex of conventional patterns,
finally, that constitutes *the* "convention" of New England historical romance—the convention in which, or
in reaction to which, Nathaniel Hawthorne wrote his
own historical fiction of Puritan New England.

Another View of Hester: Hawthorne's Heroines and the Convention

In Hawthorne's fiction of Puritan New England, as
compared to that of his contemporaries, women are
relatively rare and relatively unimportant. To be sure,
the exception to this statement—*The Scarlet Letter*—
is a major exception. But in the short tales examined in
Chapters One and Three women play subordinate
roles. They function mainly as symbols of the bonds
of human sympathy rejected by such misanthropes as
Parson Hooper or Young Goodman Brown. These
women, in all their docility and submissiveness, are the
very antithesis of the high-spirited natural heroines of
Hawthorne's contemporaries. Yet one of Hawthorne's
first published works, appearing in the Salem *Gazette*
in 1830, was a biographical sketch of the greatest
female rebel of them all, Anne Hutchinson. Like Hope
Leslie or Naomi Worthington, Mrs. Hutchinson stands
before a gathering of stern Puritan judges. This is the
conventional situation of the natural heroine. But it is
important to note how completely, in "Mrs. Hutchinson," Hawthorne reverses the meaning of this conventional situation. Rebellion, for Hawthorne, is a noble

thing in a severe Endicott or a patriarchal Gray Champion. In a Mrs. Hutchinson it is a quality to be attacked in horror. Anne Hutchinson's judges, in Hawthorne's view, are not persecutors, but rather exemplary founding fathers—"those blessed fathers of the land, who rank in our veneration next to the evangelists of Holy Writ" [223]. Mrs. Hutchinson draws her strength from the conventionally appropriate psychological source. "Her heart," Hawthorne writes, "is made to rise and swell within her, and she bursts forth into eloquence." But her eloquence is not that of an innocent Naomi or Hope Leslie. "There is a flash," we are told, "of carnal pride half hidden in her eye, as she surveys the many learned and famous men whom her doctrines have put in fear" [224].

The sources of Hawthorne's hatred of Mrs. Hutchinson are not hard to find. Left fatherless and brotherless at the age of four, Hawthorne grew up surrounded by women. Not surprisingly, he seems to have found it difficult to maintain his masculine identity in these surroundings. All his life he resented any attempt on the part of women to do a man's work, to challenge his distinct role as a male. He particularly disliked female reformers and writers—including apparently his sister-in-law, Elizabeth Peabody, and Margaret Fuller. It is of such women, and not of American "liberty," that Hawthorne's Mrs. Hutchinson is the type. "There are portentous indications," Hawthorne writes in the first paragraph of the sketch, "changes gradually taking place in the habits and feelings of the gentle sex, which seem to threaten our posterity with many of those public women, whereof one was a burden too grievous for our fathers" [217]. Hawthorne's attacks on female writers in his letters to Ticknor and Fields in the 1850's have become notorious.[14] But already in 1830 we can see the same sentiments, along with the personal anxiety of the young writer that lies behind them. "As yet," Hawthorne continues in the opening paragraph of the sketch, "the great body of American women are a domestic race; but when a continuance of ill-judged incitements shall have turned their hearts away from the fireside, there are obvious circumstances which will render female pens more numerous and more prolific than those of men, though but equally encouraged; . . . the ink-stained Amazons will expel their rivals by actual pressure, and petticoats wave triumphantly over all the field" [218]. As opposed to this despised race of man-threatening women, Hawthorne had an ideal of feminine loveliness and domesticity—that is to say of subordination—which was exemplified, so he thought, by his wife, Sophia. But Hawthorne had the ideal long before he met Sophia in 1838. He writes at the close of the first paragraph of "Mrs. Hutchinson" that "woman, when she feels the

[14] Perhaps the best known of these attacks is the contention, in a letter to Ticknor, that "America is now wholly given over to a d——d mob of scribbling women." (*Letters of Hawthorne to William D. Ticknor, 1851-1864*, 2 vols., Newark, N.J., 1910, I, 75.) Even more picturesque is the protest written to Fields (December 11, 1852): "*All* women, as author's [*sic*], are feeble and tiresome. I wish they were forbidden to write, on pain of having their faces deeply scarified with an oyster shell." ("Letters from Nathaniel Hawthorne to James T. Fields," MS Copies by Several Hands. By permission of the Harvard College Library.)

impulse of genius like a command of Heaven within her, should be aware that she is relinquishing a part of the loveliness of her sex, and obey the inward voice with sorrowing reluctance, like the Arabian maid who bewailed the gift of prophecy" [218-19].

Hawthorne was not, in short, predisposed to treat rebellious or self-willed women in the conventional manner. Like the Quaker Catharine in "The Gentle Boy," Mrs. Hutchinson follows the dictates of her heart at the expense of her domestic obligations. Of course many of Hawthorne's contemporaries, notably Mrs. Lee, were aware of the excesses of Anne Hutchinson and the Quakers. But the fact remains that they regarded these faults as excesses, as errors which did not invalidate the essence or principle of female self-assertion as represented by their heroines. For Hawthorne it was the very essence or principle that was to be deplored. The chief manifestation of the conventional heroine's rebelliousness was to love and marry a man of whom her father and her society did not approve. Her rebelliousness led quite naturally to marriage. For Hawthorne such rebelliousness is by its very nature incompatible with the subordinate role and domestic obligations of the wife. Catharine abandons her child. And Hawthorne is convinced that Mrs. Hutchinson's marriage cannot have been natural. The husband, Hawthorne insists, must have been "(like most husbands of celebrated women) a mere insignificant appendage of his mightier wife" [255]. Marriage and femininity were absolutely antithetical to feminism. Thus Hawthorne wrote rather nastily, in 1855, to his maiden sister-in-law, the reformer: "the conjugal relation is one which God never meant you to share, and which therefore He apparently did not give you the instinct to understand."[15]

In *Hope Leslie* the natural heroine is contrasted with Esther Downing, who "attained the age of nineteen," so we are told, "without one truant wish straying beyond the narrow bound of domestic and religious exercises" [I, 198]. It is important to note that Hawthorne's ideal woman has a good deal more in common with Esther Downing than with Hope Leslie, and that in his stories the characteristics of Hope—"this having our own way" [II, 68]—inevitably lead to evil consequences. Hawthorne would certainly have sided with Esther in declaring to Hope, "You do allow yourself too much liberty of thought and word: you certainly know we owe implicit deference to our elders and superiors; we ought to be guided by their advice, and governed by their authority" [I, 262]. Hawthorne's female rebels, disregarding this sort of advice, become as extreme in their fanaticism as a Parson Hooper or a Young Goodman Brown. If Hooper and Brown reveal their inhumanity by repudiating such "domestic" women as Elizabeth and Faith, Mrs. Hutchinson and Catharine reveal their inhumanity by refusing to *be* such women. They are indelicate because they are insubordinate. The young woman's defiance of authority,

[15] Quoted by Mark Van Doren, *Nathaniel Hawthorne*, New York, 1957, pp. 106-107.

great emblem of liberty in the conventional historical romance of New England, is for Hawthorne an emblem of the very worst in female pride.

Twenty years separate the publication of *The Scarlet Letter* from the publication of "Mrs. Hutchinson." But the romance begins with the same conventional situation—a proud woman stands before her stern Puritan judges.[16] And Hawthorne seems to have his 1830 heroine very much in mind: the rosebush beside the prison door from which Hester emerges is associated, in the first chapter, with "the sainted Ann Hutchinson" [48]. This phrase suggests that Hawthorne's attitude toward Anne Hutchinson and her kind may have softened since the 1830's. Hester is certainly treated with greater sympathy than Mrs. Hutchinson, and her judges are both more harsh and less qualified than were the Puritans of the 1830 sketch. But one should be careful to avoid exaggerating Hawthorne's sympathy with his heroine. A popular reading of *The Scarlet Letter* sees it as a tragedy of true love crushed by an unfeeling society. This line of criticism, in a curious way, turns Hester completely into a conventional natural heroine, unjustly persecuted by an intolerant society. But it falsifies the reality of the book. Hawthorne may pity Hester, he may sympathize with

[16] In a recent article on *The Scarlet Letter* John C. Stubbs has also noted briefly the resemblance between Hester's situation and that of the conventional romance heroine—"the situation of the heroine with a warm, loving nature alienated from, or in conflict with, Puritan severity." ("Hawthorne's *The Scarlet Letter*: the Theory of the Romance and the Use of the New England Situation," *PMLA*, LXXXIII [1968], 1445.)

her, but he does not accept her values as his own. She is not his spokesman in the book. Hawthorne's position is made quite clear, not only in his frequent criticisms of Hester, and in the seriousness of her crime, but also in Hester's voluntary return to Boston at the close. This is not the same woman who proudly maintained herself on the scaffold, who passionately exhorted Dimmesdale to flee.

It is of crucial importance to note that what Hawthorne approves in his heroine is not her rebelliousness, however splendid that quality may sometimes seem, but rather her ability to *overcome* that rebelliousness and assume the feminine qualities of domesticity. For the great difference between Hester and Hawthorne's earlier female outcasts is that Hester returns to her obligations and subordinate position. Unlike Catharine in "The Gentle Boy," Hester Prynne does not abandon her child. Hawthorne surely agrees with Dimmesdale's argument, at Bellingham's mansion, that there is "a quality of awful sacredness in the relation between this mother and this child." Hawthorne believes with Dimmesdale that the child was meant, "above all things else, to keep the mother's soul alive, and to preserve her from blacker depths of sin into which Satan might else have sought to plunge her!" [114].

What these "blacker depths" are is made clear in Chapter XIII, entitled "Another View of Hester." Hester, we learn, is on the verge of falling into feminism, into an open defiance of tradition and authority.[17] "The

[17] Hester's relationship to nineteenth-century feminism has been noted by a number of critics. See, for example, Neal F. Double-

world's law," we are told, "was no law for her mind" [164]. Hester envisions a change in the role of women, a change Hawthorne regards with horror. For with this change, Hawthorne insists, "the ethereal essence, wherein [woman] has her truest life, will be found to have evaporated" [165-66]. Hester risks being transformed permanently into a Catharine or an Anne Hutchinson. "She might," Hawthorne writes, "have come down to us in history, hand in hand with Ann Hutchinson, as the foundress of a religious sect. She might, in one of her phases, have been a prophetess. She might, and not improbably would, have suffered death from the stern tribunals of the period, for attempting to undermine the foundations of the Puritan establishment" [165]. All this might have happened, we are told, "had little Pearl never come to her from the spiritual world." Hester is saved by Pearl. "Providence," Hawthorne continues, "in the person of this little girl, had assigned to Hester's charge the germ and blossom of womanhood, to be cherished and developed amid a host of difficulties" [165]. Like Catharine in "The Gentle Boy," Hester has a choice between following the whims of her fancy or following her duties as a mother. But unlike Catharine she chooses the latter. No more than "Mrs. Hutchinson" does *The Scarlet Letter* glorify female self-assertion. To the extent that Hester forges something positive out of the aftermath of her sin, her success represents a triumph not of rebellion but of subordination.

---

day, "Hawthorne's Hester and Feminism," *PMLA*, LIV (1939), 825-28.

THE ETHIC EMBODIED in the conventional natural heroine is, at least by implication, profoundly revolutionary. The historical romancers of New England would, so it seems, set up nature over civilization, the heart over the head, impulsive youth over sober age. And yet the writers who propounded this revolutionary ethic were themselves usually quite conservative—in general outlook and often in political belief as well. One would expect such people to *fear*, rather than recommend, the triumph of nature and the heart. How, one wonders, did they deal with the possibility that the abandonment of restraint—of civilization or of reason—might lead not to progress but to chaos? How, in short, could civilization follow nature without running the risk of destroying itself?

Most of the great writers of this period—Cooper and Melville for example—were agonized by this problem. For them "the problem of American self-recognition" became, as Perry Miller has put it, "essentially an irreconcilable opposition between Nature and civilization—which is to say, between forest and town, spontaneity and calculation, heart and head, the unconscious and the self-conscious, the innocent and the debauched."[18] But the lesser writers had a way of get-

[18] Perry Miller, "The Romantic Dilemma in American Nationalism and the Concept of Nature," *Nature's Nation*, p. 199. In this article Professor Miller also speculates on the reasons why these are particularly American oppositions. "The crucial difference between the American appeal to Romantic Nature and the European," he writes, is that "in America, it served not so much for individual or artistic salvation as for an assuaging of national anxiety" (p. 203). The European turned to nature as an individual fleeing civilization. The American wanted his whole civiliza-

ting around this contradiction—a kind of semantic trick that allowed them to follow something called "nature" without braving the hazards of excess. These writers simply assumed that there were two kinds of nature, two ways of following the heart. We can see this sort of distinction in Mrs. Lee's two kinds of Quakerism— which are, finally, two kinds of religion of the heart. In the actual Quakers Mrs. Lee embodies the real dangers of obeying impulse without restraint. "The principle of their religion," she writes in *Naomi*, "flattered self-esteem and fostered spiritual pride" [336]. And yet in the heroine exactly the same "principle" is somehow purged of its dangerous connotations. Naomi "held nothing in common with the Quakers of that day," we are told, "but the essential principle of their faith" [336]. Mrs. Lee's curiously contradictory use of the word "principle" makes it clear that for her at least the dangers of excess were overcome—or evaded—by distinguishing between two sorts of impulse, two ways of following the heart, one dangerous and the other somehow safe.

Similarly there are two kinds of "nature" in these books—one wild and therefore (like the Quakers) dangerous, the other tame and therefore safe. It is the latter that is associated, in these romances, with the natural heroine. It is to this tame nature that Mrs. Lee refers when she says of Naomi that "Nature had endowed her with a vigorous reason, a strong good-sense" [41]. Book after book draws the important distinction

---

tion to flee with him, and his effort was thus, on every level, fraught with contradictions.

between the forest, on the one hand, and the meadow or garden on the other—between wild nature and the "natural." Catharine Sedgwick deals with this distinction in *Hope Leslie* by means of a device much honored in nineteenth-century romance, though for some reason relatively rare in the historical romance of New England. Hope's rebelliousness is brought out by contrast with the obsequiousness of Esther Downing. But Hope is also contrasted with another girl, an Indian named Magawisca. Magawisca grows up with the hero, Everell Fletcher, and at one point saves his life. But such a match is obviously out of the question. Magawisca finally leaves Boston for good before the marriage of Everell with the true heroine, Hope Leslie. For as Hope represents the safe "nature" of the natural heroine, so Magawisca is marshaled forth to represent the perils of the forest, of wild "nature." Just as there are two kinds of nature, so there are two kinds of heroine: fair and dark, Scott's Rowena and Rebecca, Cooper's Alice and Cora, Melville's Lucy and Isabel. The dark heroine (like Mrs. Lee's Quakers) represents the nature that cannot be reconciled with civilization, the nature that cannot safely be followed. Everell Fletcher, in *Hope Leslie*, turns from the dark Magawisca to marry Hope. Since marriage is always the final symbol of the new civilization in these books, the hero cannot marry the dark heroine. But he can reconcile civilization with the other kind of "nature" simply by marrying the fair natural heroine, the blonde. There is something terribly tenuous and circular about all this: the blonde is both "safe" and "natural" because she is *by definition* both "safe" and "natural." She represents not the resolution of a contradiction but the longing for such a resolution. But she is still important, because so many of these authors treat the longing as an accomplished fact. Thus for Catharine Sedgwick there is no danger of chaos at the end—no danger that the whim of Hope Leslie, our only guide after rejecting all the wisdom of Boston, may lead us only farther astray. Her nature is tame, and therefore safe.

Hawthorne thoroughly repudiates this convention in *The Scarlet Letter*. But his repudiation is carried out by means of the very symbols that other writers used to *support* the convention. Thus Hawthorne does not simply ignore the conventional opposition of fair and dark heroine; he subverts it by making Hester, his natural heroine, dark rather than fair. He does not reject the conventional association of the heroine with nature. Rather he radically subverts the meaning of this association: he attacks the cult of nature through the figure usually used to support it. And Hawthorne does not reject the ideas of civilization and nature that so perplexed his contemporaries; he does not ignore the question of whether civilization should (or could) follow nature. The difference is that he answers this question so unequivocally in the negative. What Hawthorne does reject, in all his skepticism, is the precarious semantic distinction between wild nature and tame nature. *All* nature, for Hawthorne, is wild. In *The Scarlet Letter* there is only the forest. There are no meadows and the only garden, with the somber exception of the graveyard, is being overrun by wild pump-kins. And as the only nature in *The Scarlet Letter* is wild, so the only heroine is dark. There are no blondes in Hawthorne's romance.[19]

The point is not that Hester is *particularly* wild, as compared with other "natural" women, but that *all* natural women are necessarily wild by virtue of their association with nature. By denying the existence of a tame nature Hawthorne is denying the whole concept represented by the blonde.[20] Hester is clearly a com-posite of blonde and brunette—both devoted mother and passionate temptress. And surely much of her im-

[19] Pearl is as close as we come to having a blonde here, but we learn that she eventually became as dark as her mother. She has, we are told, "hair already of a deep, glossy brown, and which, in after years, would be nearly akin to black" [101].

[20] But if Hawthorne has rejected the blonde in *The Scarlet Letter* why, one might ask, does he return to her with Phoebe in *The House of the Seven Gables*, and to the blonde-brunette pairing in *The Blithedale Romance*, *The Marble Faun*, and the unfinished *Septimius Felton*? It is usually argued that the blondes of *The Blithedale Romance* and *The Marble Faun* are to some extent paro-dies of the convention—which somewhat removes from Hawthorne the onus of mere conventionality. But it seems to me that we can-not so easily remove this onus. I think that Hawthorne, in many respects, *does* become more conventional in the works that follow *The Scarlet Letter*. Many conventional symbols are simply taken over and used uncritically in these later works. It is certainly true, as we will see in the next chapter, that *The House of the Seven Gables* is much more conventional than *The Scarlet Letter*. The appearance of Phoebe, exemplar of a convention examined so criti-cally only a year before, is one of a number of ways in which *The House of the Seven Gables* represents a falling off from the inten-sity and clear-headedness of Hawthorne's masterpiece. (For a dis-cussion of Hawthorne's blondes see Virginia Ogden Birdsall, "Hawthorne's Fair-Haired Maidens: the Fading Light," *PMLA*, LXXV [1960], 250-56.)

pact results from combining these characteristics in an age so firmly committed to distinguishing them. For if the natural heroine was really a temptress, then following nature could be a dangerous business indeed. If all nature was wild, then, following the conventional iconography to Hawthorne's anti-conventional conclusion, all natural heroines must have been dark. As Hester counsels freedom and escape in the forest, it is crucial to note that her dark, glossy hair is there to warn us that all is *not* well, that her advice is suspect, that the forest path is dangerous.

The forest scene, the climactic moment of *The Scarlet Letter*, is also the moment at which Hawthorne is most clearly subverting the convention—letting its own imagery throw its deepest values into question. It is extraordinary how nearly this scene seems to follow the convention. Dimmesdale, true to his role as hero, even as he violates one of Hawthorne's deepest prejudices, subordinates himself utterly to Hester. This conventional subordination of hero to heroine becomes as well the emblem of the conventional victory of heart over head. "Think for me, Hester!" Dimmesdale cries, significantly pressing his hand to his heart as he does throughout the book. "Thou art strong. Resolve for me!" [196]. When she has convinced Dimmesdale to flee with her Hester becomes in appearance the innocent natural heroine. "There played around her mouth," Hawthorne writes, "and beamed out of her eyes, a radiant and tender smile, that seemed gushing from the very heart of womanhood. . . . Her sex, her youth, and the whole richness of her beauty, came back from what men call the irrevocable past, and clustered themselves, with her maiden hope, and a happiness before unknown, within the magic circle of this hour" [202].

Here, to digress for a moment, we can see how Hawthorne has fused his own themes with his critique of the convention. For these qualities of "richness" and "beauty" are at once the conventional qualities of the natural heroine and the qualities of life whose exclusion from New England Hawthorne treats in story after story. In his earlier tales Hawthorne examines the traits of the New England character that caused it to reject, to cut itself off from, the richness and beauty of English life. This is also an important theme in *The Scarlet Letter*. But Hawthorne is also, in *The Scarlet Letter*, approaching this same question from another point of view. As he does more briefly in the young couple in "The Maypole of Merry Mount" so here, too, he examines the characteristics of the European life style itself which inevitably exclude it from the American future. Edith and Edgar, who at the outset of their story represent the life style of the "flower decked" Anglican, function in much the same way as the rebellious young couple of the convention—except, of course, for the outcome of their rebellion. Similarly Hester Prynne, the representative of richness and passion, is also the natural heroine. In revealing the inconsistencies embodied in this conventional figure Hawthorne is also, finally, showing why Hester has to deny the values of the convention in order truly to become an American.

Hester's passionate rebellion, like that of the conventional heroine, finds its equivalent in the joyous gaiety of nature:

And, as if the gloom of the earth and sky had been but the effluence of these two mortal hearts, it vanished with their sorrow. All at once, as with a sudden smile of heaven, forth burst the sunshine, pouring a very flood into the obscure forest, gladdening each green leaf, transmuting the yellow fallen ones to gold, and gleaming adown the gray trunks of the solemn trees. The objects that had made a shadow hitherto, embodied the brightness now. The course of the little brook might be traced by its merry gleam afar into the wood's heart of mystery, which had become a mystery of joy.

Such was the sympathy of Nature—that wild, heathen Nature of the forest, never subjugated by human law, nor illumined by higher truth—with the bliss of these two spirits! [202-203]

Here again Hester is differentiated from the conventional heroines, not by what she represents—for she is as natural as they are—but by Hawthorne's judgment of what she represents. There is no tame nature for Hester. There is only the "wild, heathen Nature of the forest." Hester's nature, like that of the conventional heroine, is "never subjugated by human law." But Hester's nature is also, as Hawthorne writes, not "illumined by higher truth." In relation to a convention that set up nature as the ultimate ethical value such a statement is heresy. What Hawthorne is saying is that there must be a balance between head and heart, between civilization and nature. And his constant implication is that the balance should tip—if it tip at all—in the direction of the head and of civilization. Hawthorne may deplore the Puritans' excessive reliance on the dictates of the head, he may pity the plight of Hester and Dimmesdale, and he may even (though hardly so much as his contemporaries) lament the excessive strictness of the magistrates. But he rejects firmly (as do both Hester and New England, finally) the extreme alternative offered by the convention—subordination of all to the heart, to romantic love, to nature.

Hawthorne thus rejects, finally, the whole notion of historical progress that lies behind so many of the works of his contemporaries. Hester Prynne, again like the conventional heroines, opposes to the severity of the Puritans, to the mistakes of the past, a glowing American vision of a new start, a liberated future. "Begin all anew!" she shouts to Dimmesdale, and her comment could apply not only to Dimmesdale's failure but to the failure of the whole American experiment; "Hast thou exhausted possibility in the failure of this one trial? Not so! The future is yet full of trial and success. There is happiness to be enjoyed!" [198]. "Let us not look back," Hester insists. "The past is gone! Wherefore should we linger upon it now!" To prove her point she removes the token of her identity from her breast and throws it among the "withered leaves." "See!" she explains, "with this symbol, I undo it all, and make it as it had never been!" [202]. Yet within nine pages Hester has had to reassume her scarlet letter, and Hawthorne's reading of the event hardly supports the notion that the future holds either happiness or liberation. "An evil deed," Hawthorne writes, "invests itself with the character of doom" [211].

Hester cannot escape her past, as she demonstrates at the close by voluntarily returning to Boston to wear the scarlet letter to her grave. The American experiment, as the opening paragraph of *The Scarlet Letter* makes clear, has failed to achieve its Utopian goals. Hawthorne sees this as the great, inescapable fact about America—as it is the full meaning of Hester's return to Boston. "An evil deed invests itself with the character of doom." Hawthorne will not accept the assurance that progress has restored, or will restore, the possibility of success. As the claims of the head or the claims of "higher truth" should control the "wild, heathen Nature of the forest," so the claims of the past, Hawthorne believed, were not lightly to be dismissed. By subverting the symbolic values of the natural heroine, Hawthorne was rejecting not simply the belief in nature or in the liberation of the heart but also the notion that history, and especially American history, were to be comprehended as the glorious triumph of nature and the heart over the past. In rejecting the assumptions behind the conventional historical romance of New England, Hawthorne was rejecting the essential pattern by which the writers of that convention understood the movement, the direction, and the nature of history.

PAST AND PRESENT

"Be of good cheer. The great book of Time is still spread wide open before us; and, if we read it aright, it will be to us a volume of eternal truth."

"Earth's Holocaust"

Yet Cunningham, who has lately seen him, assures me that there is now and then a touch of the genius,— a striking combination of incident, or a picturesque trait of character, such as no other man alive could have hit off,—a glimmer from that ruined mind, as if the sun had suddenly flashed on a half-rusted helmet in the gloom of an ancient hall. But the plots of these romances become inextricably confused; the characters melt into one another; and the tale loses itself like the course of a stream flowing through muddy and marshy ground.

"P.'s Correspondence"

I N THE STRICTEST SENSE, the story of Hawthorne's
treatment of seventeenth-century New England ends
with *The Scarlet Letter*. After 1850 the Puritan past,
when it appears at all in Hawthorne's fiction, is sub-
ordinated to more immediate concerns. This is not to
say that Hawthorne's concern with the New England
Puritans vanishes. The Puritans stand very significantly in the historical background of *The House of the
Seven Gables*, the unfinished English romance that
survives as *The Ancestral Footstep* and *Doctor Grimshawe's Secret*, and even of *The Blithedale Romance*.
Still, for all its significance, Puritan history is only in
the background in these books. Hawthorne does not,
after 1850, significantly deepen or broaden his understanding of seventeenth-century New England history.

But there is an important development, which becomes dominant after *The Scarlet Letter*, in the nature
of Hawthorne's *approach* to the past—in the nature of
the preoccupations which Hawthorne brings to his
treatment of the past. The easiest way of describing
this development is to say that after *The Scarlet Letter*
Hawthorne's concern with the past becomes increasingly subjective. In his tales of Puritan New England
and in *The Scarlet Letter* Hawthorne is primarily concerned with the past as *object*, as it happened, on its
own terms. In certain contemporaneous sketches and
prefaces, however—notably the "Custom-House" preface to *The Scaret Letter*—Hawthorne introduces sub-

jective historical concerns, most especially the question of his own relation to his historical material. Up through the writing of *The Scarlet Letter* these concerns of the prefaces do not enter very significantly into Hawthorne's *fiction* of Puritan New England. Beginning with *The House of the Seven Gables*, however, Hawthorne becomes more and more concerned in his fiction with ideas that grow not out of the seventeenth-century record but out of his own position as a nineteenth-century American confronting that record. Hawthorne becomes increasingly concerned with the relation between past and present, and it is in this context, in his later fiction, that he deals with the Puritan past.

The increasing subjectivity of Hawthorne's later historical fiction leads to yet another development. Through *The Scarlet Letter* Hawthorne's tales of the Puritans are "historical" in the sense that they are attempts to understand the past. Hawthorne is not interested, in these tales, with understanding the more general theoretical nature of history. He is concerned with the nature of the past, not the nature of time. But after *The Scarlet Letter* Hawthorne's historical themes become increasingly theoretical; he does become interested with understanding the nature of time. The later fiction is dominated by a dialectical debate over the "shape" of history—a debate over whether history is cyclical or linear. It is the function of this Epilogue to trace this development in Hawthorne's historical thought, to show its relation to the subjective concerns of the earlier sketches and prefaces, and to show how

194

both these developments affect Hawthorne's treatment of the seventeenth-century past.

Subjective History: The Sense of the Past

It was a commonplace of aesthetic theory, in Hawthorne's America, that the beauty of a work of imagination lay not in the artist's material but in the psychological "associations" which that material set off in the artist's mind. An artist "spiritualized" an object of contemplation by surrounding that object, in his imagination, with a train of appropriate "associations." This doctrine was summed up by Archibald Alison, who was widely influential in America, in his *Essays on the Nature and Principles of Taste* (1790). "Matter," wrote Alison, "is not beautiful in itself, but derives its beauty from the expression of the mind."[1] "Beauty" was essentially subjective, an expression of the artist's mind. As Washington Irving wrote in his 1848 preface to *Knickerbocker's History of New York*, it was the task of the American writer "to clothe home scenes and places and familiar names with those imaginative and whimsical associations so seldom met with in our new country, but which live like charms and spells about the cities of the old world." Irving boasted of his own achievement in *Knickerbocker's History*: "I

[1] Quoted in William Charvat, *The Origins of American Critical Thought, 1810-1835*, Philadelphia, 1936, p. 50. One might compare another statement of Alison's: "When the material qualities cease to be significant of the associated qualities, they cease also to produce emotion." (*Ibid.*, p. 49.) For a detailed discussion of the impact of associational psychology on conventional American aesthetic theory, see especially Charvat's third chapter, "Sources in Scottish Philosophy, Aesthetics and Culture."

have opened a vein of pleasant associations and quaint characteristics peculiar to my native place."[2]

For the historical writer the aesthetic theory of associations had a special meaning. A scene was associated, above all, with its past—with the important or pathetic events which it had witnessed at earlier times. A certain kind of romantic writer, of which Irving is an excellent example, functioned as a kind of sensitive tourist, recording his subjective psychological responses to scenes rich, as Geoffrey Crayon wrote of Europe, with "the charms of storied and poetical association."[3] For such a writer "history," like "beauty," was essentially subjective. History did not consist of a record of past events. It consisted, rather, of an imaginative evocation of the historical associations of present scenes and objects. For such a writer there was a more or less standard form for "historical" meditation. One began in the present, in contemplation of some significant scene—perhaps the birthplace of a famous writer. One then moved into a reverie of historical associations—often, when appropriate, in the form of a local legend. One then usually returned to the present. It was thus, to use Alison's words, that history served the purposes of romantic imagination by adding "beauty" to a scene through the "expression of the mind."

[2] *The Works of Washington Irving* (New Edition, Revised), 16 vols., New York, 1859, I, xiii, xiv. For a discussion of the importance of associational psychology and aesthetics to Irving, see William L. Hedges, *Washington Irving: An American Study, 1802-32*, Baltimore, Md., 1965, especially pp. 107-108, 118-19.

[3] Irving, *Works*, II (*The Sketch Book*), 10.

The formula of historical meditation, based on the doctrine of associations, was every bit as important for Hawthorne as for Irving. Such a story as "The Great Carbuncle" (1837) may be an allegory of human vanity. But it is also an effort to develop the imaginative possibilities of an Indian legend and to "associate" these imaginative possibilities with the scenery of Maine. Thus the story ends very much in the vein of Irving, the "vein of pleasant associations and quaint characteristics peculiar to my native place." "Some few," writes the narrator at the close of "The Great Carbuncle," "believe that this inestimable stone is blazing as of old, and say that they have caught its radiance, like a flash of summer lightning, far down the valley of the Saco. And be it owned that, many a mile from the Crystal Hills, I saw a wondrous light around their summits, and was lured, by the faith of poesy, to be the latest pilgrim of the GREAT CARBUNCLE" [191].

In certain moods Hawthorne is positively addicted to developing the associations of historically significant objects. "A Virtuoso's Collection" (1842), describing an imaginary museum, is little more than a list of such objects—all the way from the golden thigh of Pythagoras to the wooden leg of Peter Stuyvesant. And Hawthorne does not confine himself to real objects. He often works up real history by "associating" it with an object he himself has made up. A classic example of this procedure is "The Antique Ring" (1843), in which a young poet creates a story about Queen Elizabeth and Essex to go along with the ring he has just given to his fiancée. The story is provided at the girl's request, and the terms of that request are interesting. "It needs nothing but a story . . . ," she says of the ring. "Not that I should be too scrupulous about facts. If you happen to be unacquainted with its authentic history, so much the better. May it not have sparkled on a queen's finger? Or who knows but it is the very ring which Posthumus received from Imogen? In short, you must kindle your imagination at the lustre of this diamond, and make a legend for it" [51]. This "making a legend" for an object is characteristic of Hawthorne. It is the procedure of the narrative framework of *Grandfather's Chair*, in which the main events of New England history are associated with the chair in which Grandfather sits as he tells the story. On a deeper level this "making a legend" for an object is also the procedure of *The House of the Seven Gables*, in which the old house becomes the central object of historical meditation. And one effect of attaching the "Custom-House" preface to *The Scarlet Letter* is to make that romance, too, a "legend" associated with an object, the scarlet A that Hawthorne finds in Surveyor Pue's packet. It is worth noting that Hawthorne's original title for the volume that was to contain *The Scarlet Letter* was *Old Time Legends*.

Another effort to exploit the legendary associations of an historical object is the framework which unites the four "Legends of the Province House" which Hawthorne published in 1838 and 1839. Hawthorne presents these tales as having been heard at the Province House in Boston, now a tavern but formerly the residence of the royal governors of Massachusetts. All the

"Legends" are set in this same mansion during the eighteenth century. Thus the whole series becomes an effort to clothe a particular home scene with historical associations. What this means in this case is that Hawthorne must turn a modern tavern into a fit object of imaginative contemplation. And there are times when he frankly confesses the difficulty of his task. "To confess the truth," he writes at the beginning of "Howe's Masquerade," "I was forced to draw strenuously upon my imagination, in order to find aught that was interesting in a house which, without its historical associations, would have seemed merely such a tavern as is usually favored by the custom of decent city boarders, and old-fashioned country gentlemen" [274]. This note of difficulty returns at the end of the story:

... I drew a long breath and looked round the room, striving, with the best energy of my imagination, to throw a tinge of romance and historical grandeur over the realities of the scene. But my nostrils snuffed up a scent of cigar smoke. ... Moreover, my gorgeous fantasies were wofully disturbed by the rattling of the spoon in a tumbler of whiskey punch, which Mr. Thomas Waite was mingling for a customer. Nor did it add to the picturesque appearance of the panelled walls that the slate of the Brookline stage was suspended against them, instead of the armorial escutcheon of some far-descended governor. A stage-driver sat at one of the windows, reading a penny paper of the day—the Boston Times—and presenting a figure which could nowise be brought into any picture of "Times in Boston" seventy or a hundred years ago. [289-90]

"In truth," Hawthorne concludes, "it is desperately hard work, when we attempt to throw the spell of hoar antiquity over localities with which the living world, and the day that is passing over us, have aught to do" [290].

In Hawthorne's subjective writings about the past—those writings in which he tries to evoke the past from significant scenes in the present—there is a characteristic contrast between the tenuous immateriality of the vision of the past and the hard materiality of the present. For instance, in "Old News" (1835) a vision of eighteenth-century Boston evoked from old newspapers is but a "spectral show" [553]. In "An Old Woman's Tale" (1830) a crowd of vague and silent ghosts returns to their former town, to be dismayed by the changes that have been made since they died, and by the solidity of the real town as compared to their own lack of substance. Again and again in Hawthorne's fiction apparitions of the past appear in the present as vague, immaterial, and feeble ghosts or "shadows." The past partakes of the immateriality of historical imagination. It partakes of the vagueness of associations, which are only ideas in the mind, as opposed to the substantiality of objects of perception.

This is not to say, however, that for Hawthorne the past is in itself immaterial. "Past" can have two rather different meanings, and it is important to distinguish between them. In the objective historical sense the "past" is a collection of facts of historical record or inference. In the subjective historical sense the "past," like the "beauty" of associational aesthetics, is a matter of individual imaginative experience. It is this latter sense that concerns us here. When Hawthorne presents

200

the "past" as being immaterial, he is referring not to the past itself but to the idea he has of it in his mind. The contrast between the immaterial past and the material present, then, is simply an extension of the central aesthetic distinction between association and object of perception—between reverie and reality.

This distinction between past reverie and present reality comes to the fore once again in "The Custom-House." Here the contrast is realized even in the structure of the house. Hawthorne moves from the reality of the business floor to the more imaginative realm of the attic, where the documents of Surveyor Pue, and the scarlet A, provide imaginative access to the past. But this access is not granted until Hawthorne leaves his position at the Custom-House. As in the Province House so here, too, imaginative musings on history vanish or melt in the face of the coarse reality of the present. "It was a folly," Hawthorne writes, "with the materiality of this daily life pressing so intrusively upon me, to attempt to fling myself back into another age; or to insist on creating the semblance of a world out of airy matter, when, at every moment, the impalpable beauty of my soap-bubble was broken by the rude contact of some actual circumstance" [37]. In the face of this materiality Hawthorne imagines an aesthetic different from his own, an aesthetic based on the material and the present, rather than on imagination and the past.[4] "A better book than I shall ever write,"

_____

[4] On the congruence of the past-present and immaterial-material oppositions in "The Custom-House" compare the statement of Larzer Ziff: "The past and present, then, enter into Hawthorne's

he says of the business world of the Custom-House, "was there; leaf after leaf presenting itself to me, just as it was written out by the reality of the flitting hour" [37]. Hawthorne never abandoned his commitment to imaginative associations to write this "better book" based on present reality. But his statement about the "better book" shows how thoroughly ingrained in his mind was the opposition between immaterial and material, association and object. And it shows how thoroughly this opposition was linked in his mind with the contrast (the essence of the historical association) between past and present.

And yet given all this rumination on history as an object of meditation, the distinction between reverie and reality is relatively unimportant in most of Hawthorne's historical fiction of New England, including the romance which follows "The Custom-House." The contrast between immaterial past and material present is a direct result of a subjective approach to history, and the subjective approach to history is simply not very important in most of Hawthorne's historical fiction of the Puritans. In the historical works up to and including *The Scarlet Letter* the fictional present is the

---

theory of experience as counterparts of the distinction between inner state and materiality; as necessary elements of the view of life which informs the actual-imaginary view of fiction." ("The Ethical Dimension of 'The Custom House,'" in A. N. Kaul [ed.], *Hawthorne: A Collection of Critical Essays*, Englewood Cliffs, N. J., 1966, p. 125.) In my discussion of Hawthorne's aesthetic ideas I am also indebted, as all students of Hawthorne must be, to F. O. Matthiessen's *American Renaissance*, New York, 1941, especially to the section, "The Imagination as Mirror," pp. 253-64.

seventeenth century, not the nineteenth. Thus the "past" of the fiction is the objective historical past, while the "past" of the prefaces is the past of historical imagination. This separation of the two kinds of past between preface and fiction holds true even when there appears to be an intimate structural relationship between preface and story, as in the case of nineteenth-century "framing" of seventeenth-century material. Even in *Grandfather's Chair* the separation between "Grandfather" and the actual historical narratives is quite distinct. And in *The Scarlet Letter* the subjective concerns of the "Custom-House" preface hardly enter the romance at all. The reader who has been prepared by "The Custom-House" for a shadowy reverie on the insubstantial past has not been prepared for the sort of novel Hawthorne has actually written.

But Hawthorne pretty much ceases to write objective historical fiction after *The Scarlet Letter*. Most obviously, he moves the fictional present into the actual present, so that in the fiction as in the earlier prefaces the seventeenth century is seen from the perspective of the nineteenth. More significantly, from *The House of the Seven Gables* on Hawthorne becomes explicitly involved in his historical fiction with the subjective historical themes that were previously confined to prefaces or to such quasi-historical sketches as "An Old Woman's Tale" or "Old News." The effects of this growing subjectivity on Hawthorne's fiction can be seen most fully in *The House of the Seven Gables* and the fragments of the unfinished English romance. But one can get a hint of these effects from a story written more than a decade before *The House of the Seven Gables*, "Old Esther Dudley" (1839).

"Old Esther Dudley" is the fourth and last of the "Legends of the Province House." The heroine of the tale is an old woman, a royalist, who remains in the Province House when Boston is abandoned by the British during the Revolution. She lives on in the mansion, imagining it to be filled at night with the ghosts of departed British dignitaries. And she awaits what she regards as the inevitable return to power of the royal governor after the Revolution. At the end of the story, when John Hancock approaches to take over the Province House in the name of the victorious United States, the old woman mistakes him for the returning Sir William Howe of her fantasies, and she welcomes him back in the name of King George. When she understands her mistake she dies in despair. In what I have been calling the objective sense, the historical meaning of this tale is quite simple. Old Esther Dudley represents the spirit of the colonial past giving way to the spirit of the American future, as represented by Hancock. For instance, Esther is described at one point as being a "perfect . . . representative of the decayed past—of an age gone by, with its manners, opinions, faith and feelings, all fallen into oblivion or scorn—of what had once been a reality, but was now merely a vision of faded magnificence" [333].

But this apparent simplicity is deceptive, and to understand the story fully one should pay attention to the final phrase of this description of Esther Dudley. She represents a "decayed past" which "had once been a reality, but was now merely a vision of faded magnificence." To say that Esther is no longer a "reality" but a "vision" is to say that she has passed into the dimension of subjective history, in which the past is indeed a "vision" rather than a "reality." Esther has become an object of historical contemplation, very much like the Province House itself, an object conducive to historical associations. And as the story proceeds, Esther comes to symbolize those historical associations themselves, and perhaps even the historical imagination which produces these associations. For unlike the Hawthorne of the "Province House" frame, who has such difficulty exercising his historical imagination, Esther has no trouble in summoning up associations of past greatness from the scenes of the present. She has no trouble in "spiritualizing" the harsh realities of the present. It is rumored that at midnight she entertains in the Province House "the shadows of the Olivers, the Hutchinsons, the Dudleys, all the grandees of a by-gone generation, gliding beneath the portal into the well-known mansion, where Esther mingled with them as if she likewise were a shade" [335]. This is precisely the sort of "vision" which Hawthorne tries to summon in the nineteenth-century Province House, with more limited success. And like the true tenuous products of historical imagination, Esther is alienated from the materiality of the present. "Living so continually in her own circle of ideas," we are told, "and never regulating her mind by a proper reference to present things, Esther Dudley appears to have grown partially crazed" [336-37].

It is very important to understand what Hawthorne is doing here. If a story like "Endicott and the Red Cross" can be described as an allegorical embodiment of Hawthorne's objective historical themes, then "Old Esther Dudley," while retaining its objective dimension, is also an allegorical embodiment of Hawthorne's subjective historical themes. In "Old Esther Dudley" characters come to represent not only opposed historical forces but also the opposed *aesthetic* forces of past reverie and present reality. And the allegorization of these ideas has a peculiar additional effect, an effect of which Hawthorne seems to be only partially aware. In an allegorical sense Esther Dudley "represents" the subjective sense of the "past"; she "represents" history as reverie. The essence of the subjective sense of the past is that it is immaterial, it has no substance. And yet the essence of allegorical representation is that an immaterial idea is made material, it is given substance—in this case in the physical presence of Esther Dudley. In literalizing the longing for the past in Esther Dudley, Hawthorne makes that longing itself literal and changes the nature of that longing. Esther Dudley, in wishing for the return of the British, is wishing ultimately that history should repeat itself, not only in her imagination but in fact. The allegorization of an aesthetic force or impulse, by objectifying that impulse, tends to turn it into a full-bodied theory of the nature of history. For old Esther Dudley, history should repeat itself, it should be cyclical.

By a similar process Hancock, who embodies the materiality of the present as distinguished from

Esther's longing for the past, comes to embody the absolute repudiation of the past, the longing for historical change at all costs. "You," he says to the old woman at the close, "have treasured up all that time has rendered worthless—the principles, feelings, manners, modes of being and acting, which another generation has flung aside—and you are a symbol of the past. And I, and these around me—we represent a new race of men—living no longer in the past, scarcely in the present—but projecting our lives forward into the future. Ceasing to model ourselves on ancestral superstitions, it is our faith and principle to press onward, onward!" [341]. The wish to return to the past in imagination becomes, when literalized in allegory, the wish to return to the past in fact. And the wish to live in the real world—which gives rise in "The Custom-House" to the notion of the "better book than I shall ever write"—becomes a full-blown assertion of the idea of progress.

Such a reading is perhaps rather ponderous for the slight fabric of "Old Esther Dudley." But the seeds of Hawthorne's later development are here. The opposition between Hancock and Old Esther Dudley is the essential opposition of Hawthorne's later historical fiction—the opposition between Maule and Pyncheon in *The House of the Seven Gables*, or the opposition between America and England in the unfinished English romance. Hawthorne's principal objective historical theme, in his fiction of Puritan New England, is the formation of the New England character in the wilderness. In "Old Esther Dudley" Hawthorne announces what will become his principal historical theme after *The Scarlet Letter*—the contrast between misty past and harsh present, between history as repetition and history as change.

Cycle and Line

Hawthorne was profoundly skeptical of his contemporaries' belief in historical progress from past to present. In fact he was skeptical of almost any sort of progress. His views on the matter can be seen in an 1839 sketch, "The Sister Years," which relates a supposed interview between a young girl, representing the just-arrived New Year, and her departing sister, the Old Year. "I have a fine lot of hopes here in my basket," declares the New Year. "They are a sort of sweet-smelling flower—a species of rose!" "They soon lose their perfume," replies the "sombre" Old Year [381]. "The wisest people and the best," the older sister tells the younger, "keep a steadfast faith that the progress of Mankind is onward and upward, and that the toil and anguish of the path serve to wear away the imperfections of the Immortal Pilgrim, and will be felt no more when they have done their office." "Perhaps," cries the "hopeful" New Year, "perhaps I shall see that happy day!" "I doubt whether it be so close at hand," answers her older sister. "You will soon grow weary of looking for that blessed consummation" [378-79].

Hawthorne's skepticism about historical progress lies at the heart of the use of the Puritan past in *The Blithedale Romance*. *The Blithedale Romance* is set, of course, entirely in the present, making it as near an approach to the "better book" of "The Custom-House" as anything Hawthorne wrote. But for all its modernity the action of *The Blithedale Romance* is filled with recollections of the Puritans. The characters meet at Eliot's Pulpit—a rock in the forest where the apostle Eliot preached to the Indians. At one point Coverdale fantasizes that to future generations he and Hollingsworth will be founding "fathers." "In a century or two," he says, "we shall every one of us be mythical personages, or exceedingly picturesque and poetical ones, at all events" [129]. And Coverdale's subsequent ruminations on the need of a cemetery before Blithedale can be a real community recall the sentence at the beginning of *The Scarlet Letter*: "The founders of a new colony, whatever Utopia of human virtue and happiness they might originally project, have invariably recognized it among their earliest practical necessities to allot a portion of the virgin soil as a cemetery, and another portion as the site of a prison" [47]. A more explicit analogy between the present action and the Puritan past occurs toward the end of the book, when Coverdale encounters Hollingsworth, Zenobia, and Priscilla in the forest, again at Eliot's Pulpit:

. . . as my eyes wandered [Coverdale writes] from one of the group to another, I saw in Hollingsworth all that an artist could desire for the grim portrait of a Puritan magistrate, holding inquest of life and death in a case of witchcraft;—in Zenobia, the sorceress herself, not aged, wrinkled, and decrepit, but fair enough to tempt Satan with a force reciprocal to his own;—and, in Priscilla, the pale victim, whose soul and body had been wasted by her spells. Had a pile of faggots been heaped against the rock, this hint of impending doom would have completed the suggestive picture. [214]

The list of specific analogies between present and Puritan past in *Blithedale* could be considerably extended.[5]

But there is a far more significant general analogy behind these particular similarities between present and past. Roy R. Male has described *The Blithedale Romance* as Hawthorne's "definitive criticism of the recurring American efforts at transformation without

---

[5] The searcher after historical analogies is tempted, especially in the light of Miles's final confession of secret love for Priscilla, to see in the names of these characters a hidden reference to the more famous Miles and Priscilla whose legendary story Longfellow elaborated in "The Courtship of Miles Standish." Unfortunately, this story (which has no basis in fact) has only been "legendary" since the publication of Longfellow's poem, and that poem was published six years after *The Blithedale Romance*. Still, Hawthorne and Longfellow were close, especially as writers. They were classmates at Bowdoin and, although not especially friendly there, by 1838 they were planning a joint collection of fairy tales. Longfellow praised *Twice-Told Tales* for its use of legendary New England material, and Hawthorne provided Longfellow with the historical idea for *Evangeline* (the same story appears in *Grandfather's Chair*). In an 1858 letter to Charles Sumner Longfellow claims that the "Courtship" was not made up, but based on a "well known anecdote." (Cecil B. Williams, *Henry Wadsworth Longfellow*, New York, 1964, p. 165.) If this "anecdote" was "well known" to Longfellow in 1858, it was probably well known to him earlier. And since Hawthorne and Longfellow exchanged, or at least discussed, literary ideas, perhaps the anecdote was well known to Hawthorne, too, before he wrote *The Blithedale Romance*. In any case, for whatever the information is worth, it is at least remotely *possible* that Hawthorne had the "historical" Miles and Priscilla in mind when he named the Miles and · Priscilla of his romance.

tragedy."[6] A. N. Kaul has characterized the pattern of *Blithedale* as "the archetypal American experience: withdrawal from a corrupt society to form a regenerate community."[7] The Blithedale experiment represents an attempt to institutionalize the same sort of "new beginning" that Hester offers to Dimmesdale in the forest. And thus the point of the persistent analogies to the Puritan past in *The Blithedale Romance* is that America itself, founded by English exiles seeking a "new beginning" in the wilderness, is just the sort of community, and failure, that Blithedale is. Like Blithedale, America is an experiment at social purity, an experiment that failed. The drawing of analogies between past and present in *The Blithedale Romance* is doubly important. It broadens the significance of the action to cover the whole American experiment.[8] And, what may be more important to our present concerns, the drawing of such analogies stresses the fact that the archetypal pattern of American experience is a *recurring* pattern. In the America of *The Blithedale Romance*—Hollingsworth's dreams of progress notwithstanding—history is cyclical.

[6] Roy R. Male, *Hawthorne's Tragic Vision*, New York, 1964, p. 139.

[7] A. N. Kaul, *The American Vision: Actual and Ideal Society in Nineteenth-Century Fiction*, New Haven, 1963, p. 199.

[8] As Professor Kaul writes: "In *The Blithedale Romance* [Hawthorne] presents the utopian experiment of Brook Farm as an extension of the Puritan tradition. The backward glance of comparison runs like a rich thread through the pattern of [*Blithedale*], making explicit the significance which the American romancer saw in this otherwise quixotic enterprise." (*Ibid.*, p. 196.) See also, above, Chapter One, n. 26.

Hawthorne was not the only historical romancer of New England to see cyclical repetition, rather than linear progress, as the pattern of American history. In the introduction to *The Salem Belle* the anonymous author also stresses fundamental analogies between the errors of the past and the errors of the present. "It is too late," we are told, "to revive the folly of witchcraft, but other follies are pressing on the community,—fanaticism in various ways is moulding the public feeling into unnatural shapes" [iv]. This introduction even turns on the conventional imagery of progress, which sees the darkness of the past as giving way to the enlightened present. "It is an age," the author writes of the *present*, "of boasted liberty and light, but it may well be doubted whether these high pretensions are any powerful defense against popular mistakes." "The elements of delusion," we are told, "always exist in the human mind" [v]. This is a far cry from James McHenry's assurance, at the close of *The Spectre of the Forest*, that after the witchcraft crisis "a new order of things commenced. Frenzy and terror gave place to confidence and good will" [ii, 242].

The analogy between past and present superstition is also drawn by Paulding in *The Puritan and His Daughter*. "It cannot be denied," he writes,

that in the present age, the credulity of science is quite equal to that of ignorance in the days of yore. The reign of superstition, if we do not err, if it has ever gone by, is about to be revived; and witchcraft and necromancy seem destined to assume the dignity of sciences. It is well for the professors of mesmerism they did not practice their impositions some two centuries ago, for they would assuredly have been brought to the stake or the gallows." [II, 187]

Paulding's affirmation of the cyclical nature of history is particularly interesting because it coexists, in *The Puritan and His Daughter*, with an apparently equally sincere belief in the progressive nature of history. "Those feelings of religious and political antipathy," Paulding writes of the hero and heroine, "which had alienated their fathers, and caused so much suffering to their children, did not take root in the soil of mutual love. It would seem that civil and religious liberty are twin sisters, and cannot be divorced from each other. Hence America—we mean the United States, the legitimate representative of the New World—is not the soil or genial clime for biogtry and persecution" [II, 267-68]. There would appear to be a real uncertainty, in Paulding's mind, about the nature of history—an uncertainty leading potentially to the contradiction between cycle and line.

But in *The Puritan and His Daughter*, and in the works of Hawthorne's other contemporaries, this contradiction is only implicit. An author may alternate between the two views of history, but no author directly faces the contradiction between these views. For Hawthorne, however, the contradiction between cycle and line had particular importance, since such a contradiction grew out of his efforts to allegorize—as in "Old Esther Dudley"—the tension between historical reverie and present-day reality. Thus Hawthorne, alone among his contemporaries, turned directly to the contradiction between the linear and cyclical views of history. The initial result of this confrontation was Hawthorne's second full-length romance, *The House of the Seven Gables*, published in 1851.

IN HIS PREFACE TO *The House of the Seven Gables* Hawthorne describes his romance as being at least in part an "attempt to connect a by-gone time with the very Present that is flitting away from us" [2]. The romance that follows is certainly Hawthorne's most sustained attempt to establish connections between Puritan past and nineteenth-century present. One is constantly confronted with connections between the two ages, as in the much-remarked resemblance between the modern Judge Pyncheon and his ancestor the Colonel, who seized Matthew Maule's land. Even witchcraft, of which the old Maules were suspected and for which their first progenitor was hanged, has a modern equivalent—the same equivalent, interestingly, as in Paulding's romance two years before. Holgrave, the last descendant of the Maules, admits that his own "faculty of mesmerism" "might have brought me to Gallows-Hill, in the good old times of witchcraft" [217]. But the most important analogy between past and present, the most pervasive connection between seventeenth and nineteenth centuries, lies in the abiding feud between Pyncheons and Maules. In both ages, Hawthorne is saying, one can see clearly the essential conflict between the opposed social forces of Pyncheon and Maule, haughty aristocrat and egalitarian democrat.

But these insistent correspondences between past and present only serve to raise the even more insistent question of the nature of the relationship of past to present. One wonders, in reading *The House of the Seven Gables*, whether the meaning of juxtaposing witchcraft and mesmerism is that they are fundamentally different or fundamentally similar. One wonders the same thing about the different historical stages— past and present—of the Maule-Pyncheon feud; and at this point the question acquires considerable significance. For one will want to know whether historical sequence is significant, or whether history is simply a changing of costume. Has the nature of the central feud changed significantly, or does history simply repeat itself?

A cyclical view of history is suggested by the "moral" Hawthorne announces in his preface, that "the wrong-doing of one generation lives into the successive ones" [2]. Guilt is transmitted through a process literally described as *repetition* of the initial sin. "We are left to dispose of the awful query," Hawthorne writes of the successive Pyncheons who lived on the land seized from Matthew Maule, "whether each inheritor of the property—conscious of wrong, and failing to rectify it—did not commit anew the great guilt of his ancestor, and incur all its original responsibilities" [20]. In a sense all of this is merely a restatement of the idea of doom in *The Scarlet Letter*: "an evil deed invests itself with the character of doom" [211]. The difference is that what in *The Scarlet Letter* was applied to the life span of a single woman is extended, in *The House of the Seven Gables*, to the full span of American history. Under Maule's curse history would seem to entail the endless repetition of past acts. Americans, like the Pyncheons in the haunted looking-glass, would seem doomed to "doing over again some deed of sin" [21].

Yet there are tokens of change in the romance as well as tokens of repetition. For example, Holgrave one day tells Phoebe Pyncheon the story of the carpenter, Matthew Maule, grandson of the original "wizard," who hypnotized and eventually destroyed the beautiful Alice Pyncheon. When he has concluded his narrative, Holgrave, a descendant of this Matthew Maule, notices that he, too, has hypnotized a Pyncheon girl, in this case Phoebe. Holgrave's power over Phoebe, Hawthorne tells us, underlining the obvious correspondence between past and present, was as dangerous "as that which the carpenter of his legend had acquired and exercised over the ill-fated Alice" [212]. But in the case of this historical correspondence the emphasis is on change rather than repetition. Unlike his carpenter ancestor Holgrave does not take advantage of his power over a beautiful young Pyncheon. Instead of destroying Phoebe, Holgrave finally marries her. This marriage is clearly intended to be contrasted with the abortive relationship of Alice Pyncheon and Matthew Maule, one hundred years before. In this case, it would appear, progress is possible; the past *can be* escaped.

And yet Hawthorne, as narrator, is generally suspicious of the idea of progress in *The House of the Seven Gables*. This suspicion can be seen in the skeptical treatment of Holgrave's hopefulness. "It seemed to Holgrave—as doubtless it has seemed to the hopeful of every century, since the epoch of Adam's grand-children—that in this age, more than ever before, the moss-grown and rotten Past is to be torn down, and lifeless institutions to be thrust out of the way, and their dead corpses buried, and everything to begin anew" [179]. Even the belief in progress, Hawthorne hints, is but a cyclically recurring historical phenomenon. What Holgrave believes has been believed in "every century, since the epoch of Adam's grand-children." Yet for all his skepticism Hawthorne does not utterly dismiss hopefulness. He qualifies his criticism of Holgrave to say that the artist's error lay not in believing in progress but only in believing in *immediate* progress. "As to the main point—may we never live to doubt it!—as to the better centuries that are coming, the artist was surely right" [180].

And however much Hawthorne intends, in *The House of the Seven Gables*, to exhibit the "character of doom," the plot of the book is actually bent on exhibiting the character of hope. The plot of *The House of the Seven Gables* is dominated by conventional devices and figures associated with historical progress. Chief among these is the comic marriage plot involving Phoebe and Holgrave.[9] This marriage represents prog-

[9] On August 27, 1837, Hawthorne made an entry in his notebook about one Philip English, "who had been persecuted by John Hathorne, of witch-time memory, and a violent quarrel ensued. . . . This Philip left some bastards; but only legitimate daughters, one of whom married, I believe, the son of the persecuting John; and thus all the legitimate blood of English is in our family." (*The*

ress not only in contrast with Matthew's treatment of
Alice Pyncheon but also in terms of its overall symbolic
function of resolving the feud between the Maules and
the Pyncheons. For what is this feud between rising
democracy and waning aristocracy but the familiar
conventional conflict between "liberty" and "tyranny"?
This opposition is thoroughly conventional even down
to Hawthorne's handling of the witch trials. Matthew
Maule, progenitor of the forces of democracy, is condemned by the society of Colonel Pyncheon, progenitor of the forces of tyranny. Hawthorne's handling of
the marriage plot is also quite conventional. The ultimate representative of liberty is not Holgrave, who
forswears his views at the close, but cheerful Phoebe.
One need not object that Phoebe is a Pyncheon any
more than one need object that the natural heroine of
the convention is often the daughter of an intolerant
Puritan. The girl by her very youth represents a new
force that will overcome the forces of tyranny as well
as the whole antagonism between liberty and tyranny.
It is thus fitting in terms of the convention, however
objectionable on other grounds, that Holgrave so completely subordinates himself and his opinions to the
guidance of Phoebe. What bothers readers quite legiti-
mately is that where Hawthorne had before either

American Notebooks by Nathaniel Hawthorne, Randall Stewart
[ed.], New Haven, 1932, p. 27.) As Professor Stewart notes, "the
story . . . may have suggested to Hawthorne, in *The House of the
Seven Gables*, the union of the hereditary foes, the Pyncheons and
the Maules, through the marriage of Phoebe and Holgrave." (*Ibid.*,
p. 288.)

ignored or, as in *The Scarlet Letter*, questioned the convention, in *The House of the Seven Gables* he seems merely to accept it.

Thus in *The House of the Seven Gables* Hawthorne turns uncritically to the great conventional symbol of progress—the triumph of light over darkness. Hawthorne's acceptance of convention here is a deliberate effort to overcome what he regarded as the excessive "gloom" of *The Scarlet Letter*.[10] In *The Scarlet Letter* the "flood of sunshine" is temporary and ultimately illusory. In *The House of the Seven Gables* it is permanent. The forces of sunshine enter with the aptly named Phoebe.[11] They suffer a momentary setback when her absence at the farm is marked by days of storm and darkness. But her return to the old house is marked by a return of sunlight. At the close the dark old house, a symbol of the wrongs of the past, is left behind as the major characters move out to the country.

[10] "I found it impossible," Hawthorne wrote to Fields concerning *The Scarlet Letter*, "to relieve the shadows of the story with so much light as I would gladly have thrown in." Thus in writing *The House of the Seven Gables*, so he wrote to Evert Duyckinck, "I suppose I was illuminated by my purpose to bring it to a prosperous close; while the gloom of the past threw its shadow along the reader's pathway." "It darkens damnably toward the close," he complained to Fields, "but I shall try hard to pour some setting sunshine over it." (First letter quoted by Randall Stewart, *Nathaniel Hawthorne: A Biography*, New Haven, 1948, pp. 94-95. Second and third letters quoted by William Charvat, "Introduction," *The House of the Seven Gables*, Columbus, Ohio, 1965, p. xxii.)

[11] "Phoebe" was also Hawthorne's familiar name for his wife, Sophia.

In apparent opposition to its narrator's sentiments about the transmission of evil, the inevitable repetition of the past in the future, the romance's conventional marriage plot asserts that the future can be free of the past. Especially in the ending, when the main characters simply walk out of the old house, Hawthorne seems to be saying that progress is possible—that the influence of the past can be left behind. Hawthorne clearly intends some sort of synthesis of repetition and change, doom and progress. The point to be made here is that he is unable to *achieve* any such synthesis, so that what comes across throughout the romance, and particularly at the close, is not any synthesis of contradictory forces, but only the contradiction between them. At the end of *The House of the Seven Gables* we are simply moved from one view of human experience in time to another very different view.

The ending is clearly the least satisfactory part of *The House of the Seven Gables*. It does not work. The comic ending ignores the tragic implications of Hawthorne's many statements about the perpetuity of evil. Another way of putting this is to say that Hawthorne's emphasis on progress, at the close, ignores his earlier insistence on historical repetition. For if progress and change are the essence of comedy, then it is the essence of tragedy that past deeds cannot be left behind in the past, that "an evil deed invests itself with the character of doom." Such, for Hawthorne, was the tragedy of New England history—that the action of an Endicott left an ineradicable mark on the New England character. But in *The House of the Seven Gables* Hawthorne oscillates between two views of history. In terms of only one of these is the ending of the romance a "happy" ending. For if history is cyclical, if it repeats itself, are we not forced to take the ending ironically? Are we not forced to see Holgrave as simply repeating the error of his wife's ancestors by establishing a new family in a new house?[12] I am not prepared to take this ending as deliberately ironic. But its ironic implications can be avoided only by ignoring all that has been said before about the perpetuity of evil—about the cyclical nature of history.

Perhaps Hawthorne felt justified in finally dismissing the idea of repetition because he had killed off its great embodiment in the romance, Judge Pyncheon. For just as the idea of progress is related to Holgrave's democratic social views, so the notion of repetition, of history as cycle, is represented by the Pyncheons, and particularly by the Judge. The resemblance of the Judge to the old Colonel, in both appearance and temperament, is remarked by many of the characters and by the narrator; and it is revealed fully by Holgrave's daguerreotype. Its historical significance is clear in Hepzibah's denunciation of the Judge as he attempts to force an interview with Clifford. "You are but doing over again," she declares to her cousin, "in another shape, what your ancestor before you did, and sending down to your posterity the curse inherited from him!"

[12] F. O. Matthiessen has written of the ending of *The House of the Seven Gables*: "In the poetic justice of bestowing opulence on all those who had previously been deprived of it by the Judge, Hawthorne overlooked the fact that he was sowing all over again the same seeds of evil." (*American Renaissance*, p. 332.)

[237]. Even in dying of apoplexy in the ancestral chair, the Judge but repeats the past. It is Judge Pyncheon's symbolic function to represent the repetition of the past in the present, to represent the cyclical or "tragic" view of history. But if the Judge represents one of the two conflicting ideas of history in the book, we can hardly say that Hawthorne resolves the conflict by killing off one of the ideas. Rather we are left, once again, with the realization that Hawthorne has finally affirmed one view of history only by ignoring the other.

The contradiction between line and cycle remains unresolved at the close; tragedy remains irreconcilable with comedy. The final marriage merely masks Hawthorne's inability, or unwillingness, to deal with the historical issues he raises in *The House of the Seven Gables*. I suggest "unwillingness" advisedly; for the ending is dominated by a refusal to entertain *any* metaphysical resolution. Such a refusal is clear in Clifford's mad speech on the train. This speech proposes, to be sure, a theory of history, but it does so only to discredit such theories by placing them in the mouth of a half-insane recluse. Clifford's nervous exuberance demonstrates Hawthorne's belief (or fear) that metaphysical speculation about history is the next thing to madness. And yet Clifford's speech, for all its madness, is addressed quite clearly to the specific problem Hawthorne himself refuses to face in *The House of the Seven Gables*. "You are aware, my dear Sir," says Clifford to a surprised fellow-passenger, ". . . that all human progress is in a circle; or, to use a more accurate figure, in an ascending spiral curve. While we fancy ourselves going straight forward, and attaining, at every step, an entirely new position of affairs, we do actually return to something long ago tried and abandoned, but which we now find etherealized, refined, and perfected to its ideal. The past is but a coarse and sensual prophecy of the present and future" [259-60]. Progress and repetition, straight line and circle, are reconciled in the figure of the "ascending spiral curve."

Clifford's speech is interesting for a number of reasons. For one thing it indicates a confusion in Hawthorne's terminology and symbolism of historical time. On the one hand, Hawthorne usually associates materiality with the present and immateriality with the past as evoked in the present. This is one of the reasons for the symbolic feebleness and spirituality of Clifford. As a poet, divorced from the world, Clifford comes to represent the unreality of the artistic imagination. And as an old man returned to a new Salem after a lifetime in prison Clifford comes to represent the unreality of the imagined past—in much the same way that Esther Dudley represents that past in "Old Esther Dudley." In fact the meaning of the Clifford-Holgrave contrast is quite similar to the meaning of the contrast between Esther Dudley and John Hancock. Esther represents the ethereality of the imagined past, as compared with the solid reality of Hancock's present.

But in Clifford's speech "ethereality" is a quality not of the past but of the present. And this "ethereal" present is contrasted to a past which is "coarse and sensual." As the imaginary past is embodied in Clifford, so this "sensual" past is embodied in Judge Pyncheon. We are told of the Judge at one point that "owing . . . to a somewhat massive accumulation of animal substance about the lower region of his face, the look was perhaps unctuous, rather than spiritual, and had, so to speak, a kind of fleshly effulgence" [116]. We are later told of the Judge that "persons of his large sensual endowments must claim indulgence, at their feeding-time" [275]. Now there is not necessarily a contradiction between the pasts represented by Clifford and Jaffrey Pyncheon. Clifford represents the "past" of subjective history, while Jaffrey represents the "past" in some objective scheme of New England history—a movement in the direction of "etherealization"—which is expressed in Clifford's speech. But although the pasts of Clifford and Jaffrey are not, strictly speaking, contradictory, it is hard to see how they are related *in Hawthorne's romance*. What has the "sensual" past to do with the "spiritual" past of historical reverie? Or, to put it another way, what has the "ethereal" present of Clifford's speech to do with the rather harsh, progressive present embodied in Holgrave? Hawthorne seems, through his symbolism, to be carrying on two virtually independent ruminations on the relation of "past" to "present."

Clifford's speech also indicates that Hawthorne did not simply dismiss speculation about the nature of history. Clifford's speech demonstrates that Hawthorne was thinking about the problem of his two views of history, line and cycle, and that he even had an idea about a possible resolution of these two views, the fig-

ure of the "ascending spiral curve." But the fact that
it is Clifford who expresses this resolution shows that
for some reason Hawthorne refused at the last minute
to grapple seriously with the historical problem raised
by the subject, the approach, and the ending of *The
House of the Seven Gables*. Hawthorne seems, in the
last analysis, to have found theoretical questions somehow terrifying or dangerous.[13]

Thus in *The House of the Seven Gables*, instead of
pursuing the direction of his own inquiry Hawthorne
falls back on the rather differently directed momentum
of romance convention. And his own romance suffers
as a result. Hawthorne is able to "connect" past and
present, in the sense that he is able to find a host of
correspondences between the nineteenth and seventeenth centuries. But he is unable or unwilling, finally,
to examine the significance of these connections. Past

---

[13] Hawthorne's distrust of the theories of reformers and their
like is made clear in "The Hall of Fantasy." "There is no surer
method of arriving at the Hall of Fantasy," he writes, "than to
throw one's self into the current of a theory" [204]. After confronting a gathering of half-crazed theorists he says to his guide:
"Come, . . . let us hasten hence or I shall be tempted to make a
theory, after which there is little hope of any man" [206].

A more relevant example occurs in *The Marble Faun*, where
Clifford's figure of the spiral—of the "return" to a higher point—
is used by Miriam to reconcile the Fall with the idea of human
progress. "He has travelled in a circle," she says of Donatello, "as
all things heavenly and earthly do, and now comes back to his
original self, with an inestimable treasure of improvement won
from an experience of pain" [434]. And here again Hawthorne's
fear of such theoretical speculation is clear—this time as expressed
in Kenyon's response to Miriam's ideas. "I dare not follow you
into the unfathomable abysses, whither you are tending . . . ," he
declares. "It is too dangerous, Miriam!" [434-35].

and present remain pieces of a puzzle that Hawthorne will not, in the year following *The Scarlet Letter*, try to assemble. Hence, at least in part, the confusion of *The House of the Seven Gables*. And hence, as well, the confusion of the late unfinished romances, in which Hawthorne found himself even more perplexingly confronted with the problem of history, of the relation of past and present.

You Can't Go Home Again

Hawthorne's later works deal obsessively with the relationship of English and American branches of old English families, and with the central fantasy of an American's return to his ancestral home. "After all these bloody wars and vindictive animosities," Hawthorne writes in the significantly titled *Our Old Home*, "we have still an unspeakable yearning towards England" [33].[14] As Consul to Liverpool, Hawthorne relates, he was continually confronted with extravagant examples of this absurd American "yearning towards England"—most notably in the form of a procession of Americans each of whom "cherished a fantastic notion that he was one of the rightful heirs of a rich English estate" [30]. After describing a number of these cases, Hawthorne concludes, "There is no estimating or believing, till we come into a position to know it, what foolery lurks latent in the breasts of very sensible peo-

---

[14] *Our Old Home*, published in book form in 1863, is a collection of essays on English life previously published in the *Atlantic* and culled from the notebooks which Hawthorne kept while he was Consul to Liverpool from 1853 to 1858.

ple" [34]. Yet "foolery" or no, this yearning is as characteristic of Hawthorne himself, as of any of the Americans he met in the course of his consulship. "I was often conscious," he admits at the close of his opening sketch, "of a fervent hereditary attachment to the native soil of our forefathers, and felt it to be our own Old Home" [57].

In the next sketch he describes a fantasy that haunted him in his trips through the English countryside—a fantasy that appears again and again in his late writings. "Almost always," he writes, "in visiting such scenes as I have been attempting to describe, I had a singular sense of having been there before." This sense, he is sure, is the result of having read so many books about England. "Yet," he continues,

the illusion was often so powerful, that I almost doubted whether such airy remembrances might not be a sort of innate idea, the print of a recollection in some ancestral mind, transmitted, with fainter and fainter impress through several descents, to my own. I felt, indeed, like the stalwart progenitor in person, returning to the hereditary haunts after more than two hundred years, and finding the church, the hall, the farm-house, the cottage, hardly changed during his long absence, . . . while his own affinities for these things, a little obscured by disuse, were reviving at every step. [82-83]

This fantasy, as Edward H. Davidson has noted, came to be associated with Hawthorne's idea that he was "the last surviving male heir of a family long absent from the old home."[15] And Hawthorne was serious

15 Edward H. Davidson, *Hawthorne's Last Phase*, New Haven, 1949, p. 16.

enough about his notion of "returning" to England to
write Fields from Liverpool in 1853, asking him to
find out from a genealogist "what part of England the
original William Hawthorne came from."[16] In England, then, Hawthorne, too, fell victim to a form of
the "fantastic notion" of reclaiming kinship with the
English branch of the American family, after two centuries of separation.

And this "fantastic notion" is the central plot idea
of Hawthorne's two unfinished English romances, *The
Ancestral Footstep* (1858) and *Doctor Grimshawe's
Secret* (1860-1861).[17] These works balance, in ever-
shifting relationships, a few basic symbols: an English

---

[16] Quoted by Davidson, *ibid.*, p. 15.

[17] Between 1858 and his death in 1864, Hawthorne worked on
four romances (in addition to *The Marble Faun*) but completed
none of them. All four survive as manuscript fragments. They are,
in order of composition: *The Ancestral Footstep* (1858), *Doctor
Grimshawe's Secret* (1860-1861), *Septimius Felton* (1861-1863),
and *The Dolliver Romance* (1863-1864). The latter two, attempts
to write a romance on the theme of immortality, fall outside the
topic of the present study. The first two, the "English romances,"
represent a sustained attempt to write a romance on the theme of
the contrast between England and America. These romances are
very closely related to the essays of *Our Old Home*, since both the
romances and the essays draw on Hawthorne's English notebooks.
In fact, Hawthorne decided to publish *Our Old Home* as a book
only after he realized that he could not turn the notebook material
into a successful romance. Thus one finds scenes and even passages, in the English romances, strongly reminiscent of scenes
and passages in the essays.

I make no attempt to describe the complicated publishing history of these romances. For this and any other information about
these late books I refer the reader to Professor Davidson's invaluable study, *Hawthorne's Last Phase*. All work on these romances
is indebted to this book, and to Professor Davidson's edition of
Doctor Grimshawe's Secret (Cambridge, Mass., 1954).

hall whose step is marked by a blood-colored mark, an "ancestral footstep"; a huge, evil-looking spider; a coffin full of golden hair; various secret cabinets and chambers; and a charitable institution (modeled on Leicester's Hospital in England) in which thirteen old pensioners subsist on a charity established two centuries before. From one revision to another, and within single revisions, characters and even large segments of the story appear, disappear, or are altered drastically. Nonetheless, the essential plot of both of these romances is very simple. A young American "returns" to England to claim (or consider claiming) an English property and title from which his original American ancestor was expelled in the seventeenth century. He may or may not decide to assert his claim; and by the end of *Doctor Grimshawe's Secret* Hawthorne has even decided that the claim shall not have been legitimate. Still, both romances deal obsessively with the "fantastic notion" that Hawthorne ridicules in *Our Old Home*. Middleton, the hero of *The Ancestral Footstep*, is captivated by Hawthorne's own "return" fantasy. He "felt," we are told, "as if he were the original emigrant who, long resident on a foreign shore, had now returned, with a heart brimful of tenderness, to revisit the scenes of his youth, and renew his tender relations with those who shared his own blood" [493]. And Hawthorne writes in the first study for *Doctor Grimshawe's Secret*: "Endeavor to give the effect of a man's leaving England 200 years ago, and coming back to see it so changed" [20]. The great subject of these two unfinished romances is the effort to reconcile the split between England and America after two hundred years, symbolized by the effort of a single young American to claim his heritage, to "renew his tender relations with those who shared his own blood."

To some extent the historical pattern of these late romances results from Hawthorne's political observations of England and America, during his consulship and after.[18] But one can easily overstate the extent to which the concerns of these romances are political and the extent to which they are the result of new ideas formulated in England. For one thing Hawthorne, in contrasting England and America, is really less interested in systems of political organization than in contrasting life styles. And Hawthorne's version of the split between England and America is not so much a product of observation in England as it is the inevitable result of the view of American history expressed in the stories of New England and in *The Scarlet Letter*. Hawthorne's reaction to England could have been predicted from any of the early tales dealing with the separation from the Mother Country. In adapting themselves to their New World environment, so Hawthorne thought, Americans became very different sorts of people from their ancestors (and cousins) in the Old World. In *Our Old Home* and the English romances Hawthorne confronts the nineteenth-century results of the events of the seventeenth century.

Thus the characteristics that distinguish America

---

[18] Such a view of Hawthorne's late writing is taken by Lawrence Sargent Hall, in his study of Hawthorne's social thought, *Hawthorne: Critic of Society*, New Haven, 1944.

from England are very much the same as those set forth in the early tales and *The Scarlet Letter*. American life, for all its energy, is thin; it lacks the deep richness of English life. Americans live on meager food; the English feed on beef. In *Doctor Grimshawe's Secret* a wan New England schoolmaster and his race are chastised by the hearty, British Dr. Grimshawe. "You do not clothe yourself in substance," the doctor comments. "Your souls are not cased sufficiently. Beef and brandy . . . would have saved you. You have exhaled for lack of them" [239-40]. Opposed to the pallor of the Americans is the "ruddiness" of the British. The hero of *Doctor Grimshawe's Secret* is told by an Anglican cleric, "Your countrymen . . . are a sallow set; but I think you must have English blood enough in your veins to eke out a ruddy tint, with the help of good English beef and ale, and daily draughts of wholesome English air" [293].

This opposition becomes thoroughly schematic. Early in *Doctor Grimshawe's Secret* an English visitor notes of two American children, "They have not the ruddiness of most English children" [40]. In *Our Old Home* even Shakespeare, as Hawthorne imagines him to have been, is "a personage of a ruddy English complexion" [127]. In *The Scarlet Letter* Hawthorne made a great point of contrasting the rosy fullness of English women (and of Hester) to the increasing paleness, the "fainter bloom," of their American counterparts. The American heroine of *The Ancestral Footstep* is described as "a slight figure, much more so than English women generally are; and, though healthy of aspect, had not the ruddy complexion . . . that is believed the great charm of English beauty" [467]. A bit later this heroine herself draws the distinction between the "delicate and fragile race" of American women and "these large-framed Englishwomen" [503]. In *Our Old Home* Hawthorne repeatedly stresses how "unlike the trim little damsels of my native land" are the "country-lasses" of England—"of sturdy and wholesome aspect, with coarse-grained, cabbage-rosy cheeks" [284]. In many earlier tales Hawthorne regrets the loss to America of the rosy richness that characterized life in England. But in England he finds that the extreme of physical richness also has its disadvantages. He describes in horror the "English lady of fifty," with her "awful ponderosity of frame, not pulpy, like the looser development of our few fat women, but massive with solid beef and streaky tallow; so that (though struggling manfully against the idea) you inevitably think of her as made up of steaks and sirloins" [66].

But if old English women are fat and beefy, old American women are "thin, careworn, and frail" [66]. What one wants, ideally, is a sort of compromise. The attempt to find such a compromise is precisely the point of the central plot of the English romances—of the tale of an American returned to England to "renew his tender relations with those who shared his own blood." In *Doctor Grimshawe's Secret* Hawthorne writes that an old pensioner in the charity hospital maintains

that history and observation proved, that all people . . . needed to be transplanted, or somehow renewed, every

few generations; so that, according to this ancient philosopher's theory, it would be good for the whole people of
England, now, if it could at once be transplanted to . . .
[America], where its fatness, its sleepiness, its too great
beefiness, its preponderant animal character, would be
rectified by a different air and soil; and equally good, on
the other hand, for the whole American people to be transplanted back to the original island, where their nervous-
ness might be weighted with heavier influences, where
their little women might grow bigger, where their thin
dry men might get a burthen of flesh, and good stomachs;
where their children might, with the air, draw in a reverence for age, forms, and usage. [101]

It is the function of the basic plot of these romances to
bring Hawthorne's fiction, in a sense, full circle—to
resolve the historical process of separation whose beginning is described in the early tales and *The Scarlet
Letter*. It is Hawthorne's hope in these late works that
his hero can somehow overcome the consequences of
the actions of an Endicott, a Gray Champion or a Bellingham, two hundred years before. For Hawthorne
has come to feel, in the 1850's, that perhaps the cost
of Endicott's defiance has been too great, perhaps the
home in the wilderness is not enough, perhaps the
American plant had better be grafted back onto the
English stock.

And new concerns of the 1850's complicate the notion of reconciliation, ultimately coming to dominate
Hawthorne's conception of the differences between
America and England. In *Our Old Home*, for instance,
an ancient oak precipitates a meditation on the different
character of time in England and America:

The man who died yesterday or ever so long ago [Hawthorne writes of England] walks the village-street to-day, and chooses the same wife that he married a hundred years since, and must be buried again to-morrow under the same kindred dust that has already covered him half a score of times. . . . Better than this is the lot of our restless countrymen. . . . Rather than such monotony of sluggish ages . . . , let us welcome whatever change may come,—change of place, social customs, political institutions, modes of worship,—trusting that, if all present things shall vanish, they will but make room for better systems, and for a higher type of man to clothe his life in them, and to fling them off in turn. [79]

America is change, progress; in England history simply repeats itself. Hence the dispute between an old Englishman and the American hero in *Doctor Grimshawe's Secret*. "The past is nothing with you," says the old man of Americans; "whereas Heaven intended it as a foundation for a present, to keep it from vibrating and being blown away with every breeze." "There is something in what you say," the young man replies; "but I would not see in my country, what I see elsewhere—the Past hanging like a millstone round a country's neck, or incrusted in stony layers over the living form; so that, to all intents and purposes, it is dead" [82]. The American is saddened to think "how generations had succeeded one another, over and over, in immemorial succession, in this little spot, being born here, living, dying, lying down among their fathers' dust, and forthwith getting up again, as it were, and recommencing the same meaningless round, and really bringing nothing to pass; for probably the generation of to-day, in so secluded and motionless a place as this, had few or no ideas in advance of their ancestors of five centuries ago" [92].

In the England and America of the late romances Hawthorne has objectified more than the opposition of Old World richness and New World pallor. He has objectified as well the conflict between opposed views of history that dominates *The House of the Seven Gables*. England is stasis, repetition; America is change. Indeed there is a great deal in Hawthorne's handling of the "missing heir" theme in the English romances that recalls *The House of the Seven Gables*. To a remarkable degree the English branch of the hero's family corresponds to the aristocratic Pyncheons, while the American branch corresponds to the democratic Maules. There is some sort of curse on the English family, as on the Pyncheons. In both cases the curse results from an initial act of dispossession—either of the American branch by the English, or of the Maules by the Pyncheons. As the Maules hold the secret that would ensure the Pyncheon claim to much greater wealth, so the American branch possesses a secret that would ensure the claim of the English family to a much higher station than they now hold in the English aristocracy. In both cases the secret involves concealed documents. In some versions of the "missing heir" story, in fact, we are told that the original American progenitor of the hero's family was—like Matthew Maule—hanged for witchcraft. But the English romances most clearly recall *The House of the Seven Gables* in their historical span, in the attempt, as Hawthorne wrote in *The Ancestral Footstep*, to bring together "the past time and the present, and the two ends of the story" [515]. And this effort necessarily brings up the old persistent question: is the present simply a repetition of the past, or is it an advance or at least a change?

Hawthorne is no more able to answer the question in the English romances than in *The House of the Seven Gables*. One could argue that he is less able to do so, since he at least managed (however unsatisfactorily) to bring *The House of the Seven Gables* to a conclusion. In the English romances change and stasis, progress and repetition are simply embodied in America and England. Hawthorne regards the embodiments, incapable of finding either resolution or compromise. At times he can praise the settled elegance of English life. At other times he can side completely with America—as in his elaboration of the "moral" of *The Ancestral Footstep*: "Let the past alone," he writes, "do not seek to renew it; press on to higher and better things,—at all events, to other things; and be assured that the right way can never be that which leads you back to the identical shapes you long ago left behind. Onward, onward, onward!" [488-89].[19] Hawthorne can alternate between these two views, but he cannot settle on one or the other.

[19] It is interesting to compare this "moral," especially in its wording, to the end of Hancock's speech to the old woman in "Old Esther Dudley." "Ceasing to model ourselves on ancestral superstitions," he says of himself and his American contemporaries, "it is our faith and principle to press onward, onward!" [341].

Each is insufficient by itself, yet it is impossible for Hawthorne to balance them.

His problem is clearest in his indecision as to what to do with his hero. Shall the hero claim his English title or shall he not? If he should claim his title he would clearly compromise his Americanness—much as Holgrave compromises his radicalism by moving into Judge Pyncheon's country house. But if the hero should renounce his claim, he would simply be admitting that there is no way of reconciling American progress with English repetition. In the midst of *Doctor Grimshawe's Secret* Hawthorne stumbles upon a way of apparently getting out of this dilemma. The hero, now named Edward Redclyffe, shall be *deluded* about his claim to the English estate. He will return to his Americanness—which he has already demonstrated by being elected to Congress—when he realizes the futility of his aristocratic yearnings. He will not have to make the decision the earlier heroes had to make, since the English estate will no longer be an option. Thus Hawthorne hopes to overcome his problem by begging—or, really, evading—the question.

But the question will not so easily be evaded, and it soon reappears in another form. Hawthorne decides that an old pensioner, in earlier drafts the primary exponent of the English point of view, will turn out to be both an American and the true missing heir. The old pensioner is thus immediately provided with a New England past and, even, an earlier appearance in the book. He also, more and more, becomes Hawthorne's

237

own spokesman in the book; the attention previously given to the young hero is increasingly turned to this old man. And, of course, the question bobs right back to the surface: what will *this* man choose, America or England? The only effect of the change in heirs, finally, is that it shifts the question from the conventional young hero to a figure who is much closer to Hawthorne, both in age and temperament.

Hawthorne toys with one more solution to the problem. The old pensioner will discover his inheritance on his deathbed and will thus perish before he has to decide anything. Even this solution gives only temporary relief, however, for the question remains unanswered. What, one wonders, *would* the old pensioner have decided? So Hawthorne chose another way of avoiding the question. He never completed *Doctor Grimshawe's Secret*. He abandoned his attempt to write an English romance about a missing American heir and set out on a new theme which would not embroil him in the old problems. But even his last two romance fragments, based on the theme of immortality, veer back toward the old theme as they begin to get cluttered up with trans-Atlantic genealogies, missing American heirs, and ancestral footsteps. Even poor Septimius Felton, in the midst of his attempt to synthesize the elixir of life, is offered the refusal of an English estate and title.

Hawthorne could neither resolve nor escape his dilemma about the relation of past and present. He might have overcome his old distinction between America and England. There might have been an international marriage, for example, Pearl come home to marry a Congressman. In a sense this is the theme James explored in his international novels.[20] But Hawthorne could no longer separate the problem of America and England from the problem of progress and stasis, line and circle. These remained, to him, irreconcilable and inescapable. The contradiction between them did not provide for him the basis of a creative impulse, as, for example, the contradiction between civilization and nature stimulated the imagination of Cooper. For Hawthorne the contradiction simply precluded successful artistic effort. *Doctor Grimshawe's Secret* remains a fragment, not even a great fragment really, but rather the pitiful record of an author's confrontation with materials that would not yield to the pressure of his intellect.

Hawthorne's effort to develop the theme of the "return" to England and the past ends, then, in confusion and failure. The failure of the English romances is partly a matter of Hawthorne's inability either to settle or to dismiss his dilemma about the nature of histori-

---

[20] Compare Harry Levin's comment on Pearl: "When we read . . . that she grew up an heiress and traveled abroad, we realize that we can pursue her further adventures through the novels of Henry James." (*The Power of Blackness*, New York, 1958, p. 78.) The relation of James's international theme to Hawthorne's fiction of New England is also suggested by Susan Stringham's reaction to London in *The Wings of the Dove*. "Mrs. Lowder's life," James writes, "bristled for [Susan] with elements that she was really having to look at for the first time. They represented, she believed, the world, the world that, as a consequence of the cold shoulder turned to it by the Pilgrim Fathers, had never yet boldly crossed to Boston." (*The Wings of the Dove*, New York, 1937 [Modern Library], I, 188.)

cal time—his inability to choose between history as line
and history as cycle. But the confusion of the English
romances is even more fundamentally a matter of Hawthorne's failure to distinguish between what I have
been calling the objective past and the subjective past.
It is not clear which of these pasts Hawthorne hopes
to recover by having his hero return to England, and
it is therefore unclear—not only to the reader but also,
apparently, to Hawthorne—what the return to England means.

In the objective historical sense the return to "our
old home" implies a return to the past *in fact*. The
hero will actually recover the qualities of "ruddiness"
and physical substantiality sacrificed to the necessities
of the wilderness. This recovery is symbolized by the
fact that the hero will also in fact recover the English
estate. Thus the ancestral mansion, symbolic generally
of "England," becomes specifically symbolic of the
physical qualities left behind by the Puritans. But in
the subjective historical sense the "return" to the past
is simply the reverie of the historical imagination in
the face of an historically significant scene. The recovery of the past is, in this sense, only imaginary.
Hawthorne in England is at once the social observer,
seeking the historical origins of American customs and
institutions, and the sensitive tourist, seeking historical
"associations." He never succeeds in reconciling these
roles, nor is he able to keep them entirely separate in
his mind.

Thus the "past" to which the hero of the English
romances returns is really two pasts. The ancestral

mansion, for instance, is both a symbol of British social and political life, and a haunted house, pregnant
with such associations as the legend of the bloody footstep. It is conceivable that Hawthorne might have
fused these two pasts. He might have made the legendary associations of the ancestral home into fit symbols
of the objective English past. This is what he is apparently trying to do—for instance, in his linking of the
bloody footstep with the departure of the Puritans
from England. But unfortunately the imaginative immateriality of the subjective past makes it almost
impossible to relate that past to an objective past
whose principal characteristic, in Hawthorne's mind, is
its "ruddy" and "beefy" substantiality. In Hawthorne's
objective view the past is "sensual" while the present
is "ethereal." In his subjective view the past is vague
and insubstantial while the present is characterized,
above all, by its hard materiality.

Hawthorne's efforts to recover the objective reality
of the English past always evaporate, in the English
romances, in the vague reverie of the subjective historical meditation. I have suggested that the old pensioner in *Doctor Grimshawe's Secret*, in addition to
becoming the true heir, also becomes to some extent
the alter ego of the aging Hawthorne. There is added
significance, therefore, in his reaction to the fantasy,
true to form for the missing American heir, that he
himself has lived since the days of King James. "An
old man," he muses, "grows dreamy as he waxes away:
and I, too, am sometimes at a loss to know whether I
am living in the past or the present, or whereabouts in

241

time I am—or whether there is any time at all. But I should think it hardly worth while to call up one of my shifting dreams more than another" [117]. Hawthorne did not stop writing at this point. But it was probably in such a mood that he put his romance of past and present aside, as simply another "shifting dream."

BIBLIOGRAPHY OF
PRIMARY SOURCES

THE FOLLOWING listing indicates the edition of each work referred to in the bracketed page references throughout this study. It also includes titles read for the study and considered to be relevant, which do not happen to be quoted. In the case that the publication date of the edition used is not the same as the date of the first edition, the latter date is indicated in brackets, following the title. In the case of Hawthorne's short stories, each listing gives the date and place of first publication.

This list could not have been compiled—indeed this study could not have been written—were it not for Lyle H. Wright's *American Fiction, 1774-1850: A Contribution Toward a Bibliography*, 2nd rev. edn., San Marino, Calif., 1969.

Bacon, Delia Salter, *Castine*, in *Tales of the Puritans*, New Haven, 1831.

———, *The Fair Pilgrim*, in *Tales of the Puritans*.

———, *The Regicides*, in *Tales of the Puritans*.

Barker, Benjamin, *Zoraida: or the Witch of Naumkeag! a Tale of the Olden Time* (published under the pseudonym of "Egbert Augustus Cowslip, Esq."), Boston, 1845.

Boston Two Hundred Years Ago, or The Romantic Story of Miss Ann Carter, Daughter of one of the first settlers, and the celebrated Indian chief, Thundersquall; with many humorous reminis-

cences and events of olden time, Exeter, N.H., 1831 [anon.] (bound in the back of an edition of Jeremy Belknap's *The Foresters*).

Cheney, Harriet Vaughan, *A Peep at the Pilgrims in Sixteen Hundred Thirty-Six. A Tale of Olden Times*, Boston, 1824.

———, *The Rivals of Acadia, an Old Story of the New World*, Boston, 1827.

Child, Lydia Maria, *Hobomok, A Tale of Early Times*, Boston, 1824.

The Christian Indian; or, Times of the First Settlers . . . First of a Series of American Tales, New York, 1825.

Cooper, James Fenimore, *The Wept of Wish-Ton-Wish. A Tale* [1829], New York, 1856.

Dawes, Rufus, *Nix's Mate: an Historical Romance of America*, New York, 1839.

Furman, Garitt, *Redfield; a Long-Island Tale of the Seventeenth Century*, New York, 1825.

Hawthorne, Nathaniel, "Alice Doane's Appeal," *Standard Library Edition of the Works of Nathaniel Hawthorne* (hereinafter *SLE*), George Parsons Lathrop (ed.), 15 vols., Boston, 1882-1891, xii (*Token*, 1835).

———, *The Ancestral Footstep, SLE*, xi.

———, "The Antique Ring," *SLE*, xii (*Sargent's New Monthly Magazine*, 1843).

———, *The Blithedale Romance, Centenary Edition of the Works of Nathaniel Hawthorne* (hereinafter *CE*), Columbus, Ohio, 1962–, iii.

————, *Doctor Grimshawe's Secret*, Edward H. Davidson (ed.), Cambridge, Mass., 1954.

————, "Endicott and the Red Cross," *SLE*, ɪ (Salem *Gazette*, 1837).

————, "The Gentle Boy," *SLE*, ɪ (*Token*, 1832).

————, *Grandfather's Chair* (*The Whole History of Grandfather's Chair*), *SLE*, ɪᴠ.

————, "The Gray Champion," *SLE*, ɪ (*New England Magazine*, 1835).

————, "The Great Carbuncle," *SLE*, ɪ (*Token*, 1837).

————, "The Hall of Fantasy," *SLE*, ɪɪ (*The Pioneer*, 1843).

————, *The House of the Seven Gables*, *CE*, ɪɪ.

————, "Howe's Masquerade," *SLE*, ɪ (*Democratic Review*, 1838).

————, "Main Street," *SLE*, ɪɪɪ (*Aesthetic Papers*, E. P. Peabody [ed.], 1849).

————, "The Man of Adamant," *SLE*, ɪɪɪ (*Token*, 1836).

————, *The Marble Faun*, *CE*, ɪᴠ.

————, "The Maypole of Merry Mount," *SLE*, ɪ (*Token*, 1836).

————, "The Minister's Black Veil," *SLE*, ɪ (*Token*, 1836).

————, "Mrs. Hutchinson," *SLE*, xɪɪ (Salem *Gazette*, 1830).

————, "Old Esther Dudley," *SLE*, ɪ (*Democratic Review*, 1839).

————, "The Old Manse," *SLE*, ɪɪ (Preface to *Mosses from an Old Manse*, 1846).

———, "Old News," *SLE*, III (*New England Magazine*, 1835).

———, *Our Old Home*, *SLE*, VII.

———, *Passages from the American Notebooks*, *SLE*, IX.

———, *The Scarlet Letter*, *CE*, I.

———, "The Sister Years," *SLE*, I (Salem, 1839, Broadside).

———, "A Virtuoso's Collection," *SLE*, II (Boston *Miscellany*, 1842).

———, "Young Goodman Brown," *SLE*, II (*New England Magazine*, 1835).

Herbert, Henry William, *The Fair Puritan, an Historical Romance of the Days of Witchcraft* (published under the pseudonym of "Frank Forrester") [1844-1845], Philadelphia, 1875. (This work first appeared as three separate, but not self-contained volumes: *Ruth Whalley: or, The Fair Puritan* [Boston, 1844], *The Innocent Witch* [Boston, 1845], and *The Revolt of Boston* [Boston, 1845].)

Lee, Eliza Buckminster, *Delusion; or the Witch of New England*, Boston, 1840.

———, *Naomi; or Boston, Two Hundred Years Ago*, Boston, 1848.

McHenry, James, *The Spectre of the Forest, or, Annals of the Housatonic, a New-England Romance*, New York, 1823.

Motley, John Lothrop, *Merry-Mount; A Romance of the Massachusetts Colony*, Boston, 1849.

Neal, John, *Rachel Dyer: A North American Story* [1828], John D. Seelye (ed.), Gainesville, Fla., 1964.

Panola: or, The Indian Sisters. Scenes in Forest Life, New York, 1849 [anon.].

Paulding, James Kirke, *The Puritan and His Daughter*, New York, 1849.

The Salem Belle: A Tale of 1692, Boston, 1842 [anon.].

Salem Witchcraft; or the Adventures of Parson Handy, from Punkapog Pond [1820], New York, 1827 [anon.]. (This work first appeared in serial form in the *New York Literary Journal and Belles-Lettres Repository* [Fall, 1820].)

Sanford, Ezekiel, *The Humors of Eutopia: A Tale of Colonial Times. By an Eutopian.* Philadelphia, 1828.

Sedgwick, Catharine Maria, *Hope Leslie: or, Early Times in the Massachusetts* [1827], New York, 1842.

Stone, William Leete, *Mercy Disborough: A Tale of the Witches*, in *Tales and Sketches, Such as They Are*, 2 vols. New York, 1834, I. (This work was published separately as *The Witches: A Tale of New England*, Bath, N.Y., 1837. My references are to *Tales and Sketches*.)

Whittier, John Greenleaf, *Legends of New England* [1831], John B. Pickard (ed.), Gainesville, Fla., 1965.

———, *Margaret Smith's Journal in the Province of Massachusetts Bay, 1678-79* [1849], in *The Prose*

BIBLIOGRAPHY OF PRIMARY SOURCES

Works of John Greenleaf Whittier, 2 vols., Boston, 1866, I.

The Witch of New England: A Romance, Philadelphia, 1824 [anon.].

INDEX

Alison, Archibald, 195, 195n, 196

Andros, Edmund, 34

associations: as principle of aesthetics, 195-196; function in historical writing, 196; importance to Hawthorne, 197-208

Austen, Jane, 160n

Bacon, Delia, *The Regicides*, 28n, 31-32, 33

Bancroft, George, 5, 7, 8, 12, 13, 34-35, 41; and Hawthorne, 50

Belknap, Jeremy, *The Foresters*, 11

Bellingham, Richard, 135-136

Birdsall, Virginia Ogden, 185n

Bodel, Jean, viii

Bradstreet, Simon, 34, 40

Bryant, William Cullen, 3-4

Burroughs, George, 101

Calef, Robert, 99n

Carlyle, Thomas, 6

Channing, William Ellery, 3-4

Charvat, William, 195n

Cheney, Harriet Vaughan, *A Peep at the Pilgrims*, 20, 23, 85n, 88, 89, 151-152, 156, 162-163, 169; *The Rivals of Adadia*, 20-21

Child, Lydia Maria, *The First Settlers of New England*, 93; *Hobomok*, 17, 87, 91, 95, 100, 151

Choate, Rufus, 4-5, 10, 13, 16

Cooper, James Fenimore, ix, x, xi, 6, 39n, 41, 181, 183, 239;

The Wept of Wish-Ton-Wish, 24-27, 28n, 29, 30, 30-31, 60, 85, 88-89, 94, 169

Cotton, John, 13, 135n

Craven, Wesley Frank, 24n, 40

Crews, Frederick C., 52, 71n, 72, 171-172

Davidson, Edward H., 227, 228n

Dawes, Rufus, *Nix's Mate*, x, 35-44, 80, 103, 104, 155, 161

Dawson, Edward, 53n, 110n

decline, idea of, 22-24, 60; Cooper and, 26-27; Hawthorne and, 22, 60-64, 137-146; relation to founding father, 23; relation to idea of progress, 23, 44; relation to idea of revolution, 42-43, 103-104

Dixwell, John, 28

Doubleday, Neal F., 179-180n

Dudley, Thomas, 18-19, 20

Duyckinck, Evert, 219n

Dyer, Mary, 97, 101

Eliot, John, 95-96

Emerson, Ralph Waldo, 4, 5

Endicott, John, 13, 18, 53, 141n; Hawthorne's treatment of, 61

English, Philip, 217n

Fiedler, Leslie, 154-155

Fields, James T., 175, 219n, 228

Fogle, Richard Harter, 77n

founding father, 20; as regicide,

251